# THE GUILT

## of SIN

## THE CHARLES G. FINNEY
## MEMORIAL LIBRARY

**Evangelistic Sermon Series**
- So Great Salvation
- The Guilt of Sin
- True and False Repentance
- God's Love for a Sinning World

**Revival Sermon Series**
- Victory Over the World
- True Saints
- True Submission

**Sermons on Prayer**
- Prevailing Prayer

# THE GUILT
## of SIN

### Evangelistic Messages

## CHARLES G. FINNEY

KREGEL PUBLICATIONS
GRAND RAPIDS, MICHIGAN 49501

*The Guilt of Sin,* by Charles G. Finney. Copyright © 1965 by
Kregel Publications, a division of Kregel, Inc. P. O. Box 2607,
Grand Rapids, MI 49501. All rights reserved. This series of
sermons selected from *Sermons on The Way of Salvation* by
Charles G. Finney.

**Library of Congress Catalog Card Number 65-25845**

ISBN   0-8254-2616-2

   7  8  9  10  Printing/Year  93

*Printed in the United States of America*

# CONTENTS

Publisher's Foreword

1. The Guilt of Sin                                    11
       Acts 17:30, 31

2. The Sinner's Doom                                   37
       Proverbs 29:1

3. When a Soul Is Lost                                 58
       Mark 8:36, 37

4. God's Anger                                         80
       Psalm 7:11

5. When Sin Is Fatal                                  103
       James 2:10; Luke 16:10

# PUBLISHER'S FOREWORD

Why this new edition of the sermons of Charles Grandison Finney? Because in many ways the days in which we are living are a duplicate of the day and situation in which Finney himself proclaimed the message which God had given him — the call to evangelism and to revival. These messages speak to our day in no uncertain sound for conditions within the church, and in the world around, call for a voice from God, a resounding clarion call for return to the Biblical standard of Christian life, and the God-ordained plan of redemption and revival.

These have been chosen and arranged with the needs of the world and church today in view. They are as applicable in this day of falling away and departure from the faith as they were in Finney's day. Heart-searching and uncompromising, they cut away the froth and frills so apparent in much modern preaching to reveal God's message for a sinning world, a world seemingly intent upon self-destruction and self-aggrandizement.

It is the publisher's prayer that these messages in their new form will convey God's message to our needy world, revealing His will and purpose for His Church — and His divine plan of salvation for an unbelieving generation.

The Publishers

# 1

# THE GUILT OF SIN

"And the times of this ignorance God winked at; but now commandeth all men everywhere to repent: because he hath appointed a day, in which he will judge the world in righteousness, by that man whom he hath ordained; whereof he hath given assurance unto all men, in that he hath raised him from the dead."—Acts xvii. 30, 31

THE text declares that God will judge the world in righteousness. I shall not at this time dwell on the *fact* that God will judge the world, nor upon the fact that this judgment will be in righteousness; but shall endeavour to ascertain what is the rule by which our guilt is to be measured; or in other words what is implied in judging the *world in righteousness*. What is the righteous rule by which guilt is measured, and consequently the just punishment of the sinner allotted?

In pursuing this subject, I shall deem it important:

I. TO STATE BRIEFLY WHAT THE CONDITIONS OF MORAL OBLIGATION ARE ; and

II. COME DIRECTLY TO THE MAIN POINT, THE RULE BY WHICH GUILT IS TO BE MEASURED.

*I. State briefly what the conditions of moral obligation are.*

1. Moral obligation has respect to the ultimate in-

tention of the mind. The end had in view, and not the mere external act, must evermore be that to which law pertains and of which guilt is predicated. Surely guilt cannot be predicated of the outward act merely, apart from intention : for if the outward act be not according to the intention, as in the case of accidents, we never think of imputing guilt ; and if it be according to the intention, we always, when we act rationally, ascribe the guilt to the intention, and not to the mere hand or tongue, which became the mind's organ in its wickedness.

This is a principle which everybody admits when he understands it. The thing itself lies among the intuitive affirmations of every child's mind. No sooner has a child the first idea of right and wrong, but he will excuse himself from blame by saying that he did not mean to do it, and he knows full well, that if this excuse be true it is valid and good as an excuse ; and moreover he knows that you and everybody else both know this and must admit it. This sentiment thus pervades the minds of all men and none can intelligently deny it.

2. Having premised so much, I am prepared to remark that the first condition of moral obligation is the possession of the requisite powers of moral agency. There must be intelligence enough to understand in some measure the value of the end to be chosen or not chosen, else there can be no responsible choice. There must be some degree of sensibility to good sought, or evil shunned ;—else there never would be any action put forth, or effort made; and there must

also be the power of choice between possible courses to be chosen. These are all most manifestly requisites for moral choice, or in other words for responsible moral action and obligation.

3. It is essential to moral obligation that the mind should know in some measure, what it ought to intend.

It must have some apprehension of the value of the end to be chosen, else there can be no responsible choice of that end, or responsible neglect to choose it. Everybody must see this, for if the individual when asked, why he did not choose a given end, could answer truly, " I did not know that the end was valuable and worthy of choice "; all men would deem this a valid acquittal from moral delinquency.

4. Supposing the individual to know what he ought to choose; then his obligation to choose it does not grow out of the fact of God's requiring it, but lies in the value of the end to be chosen. I have said that he must perceive the end to be chosen, and in some measure understand its value. This is plain. And this apprehension of its value is that which binds him to choose it. In other words, the moral law which enjoins love, or good willing must be subjectively present to his mind. His mind must have a perception of good which he can will to others, in connection with which a sense of obligation to will it springs up, and this constitutes moral obligation.

These are substantially the conditions of moral obligation ; the requisite mental powers for moral action ; and a knowledge of the intrinsic value of the good of being.

Before leaving this topic, let me remark that very probably, no two creatures in the moral universe have precisely the same degree of intelligence respecting the value of the end they ought to choose ; yet shall moral obligation rest upon all these diverse degrees of knowledge, proportioned ever more in degree to the measure of this knowledge which any mind possesses. God alone has infinite and changeless knowledge on this point.

*II.* I come now to speak *of the rule* by which the guilt of refusing to will or intend according to the law of God must be measured.

1. Negatively, guilt is not to be measured by the fact that God who commands is an infinite being. The measure of guilt has sometimes been made to turn on this fact, and has been accounted infinite because God whose commands it violates is infinite. But this doctrine is inadmissible. It lies fatally open to this objection, that by it all sin is made to be equally guilty, because all sin is equally committed against an infinite being. But both the Bible and every man's intuitive reason proclaim that all sins are not equally guilty. Hence the measure or rule of their guilt cannot be in the fact of their commission against an infinite being.

2. Guilt cannot be measured by the fact that God's authority against which sin is committed is infinite. Authority is the right to command. No one denies that this in God is infinite. But this fact cannot constitute the measure of guilt, for precisely the reason just given—namely, that then all sin becomes equally guilty, being all committed against infinite authority ;

which conclusion is false, and therefore the premises are also.

3. The degree of guilt cannot be estimated by the fact that all sin is committed against an infinitely holy and good being; for reasons of the same kind as just given.

4. Nor from the value of the law of which sin is a transgression; for though all admit that the law is infinitely good and valuable, yet since it is always equally so, all sin by this rule must be equally guilty—a conclusion which being false, vitiates and sets aside our premises.

5. The rule cannot lie in the value of that which the law requires us to will, intend or choose, considered apart from the mind's perception of the value; for the intrinsic value of this end is always the same, so that this rule too, as the preceding, would bring us to the conclusion that all sins are equally guilty.

6. Guilt is not to be measured by the tendency of sin. All sin tends to one result—unmingled evil. No created being can tell what sins have the most direct and powerful tendency to produce evil; since all sin tends to produce evil and only evil continually. Every modification of sin may for aught we know tend with equal directness to the same result—evil, and nothing but evil.

7. Guilt cannot be measured by the design or ultimate intention of the sinner. It does indeed lie in his design and in nothing else; yet you cannot determine the amount of it by merely knowing his design; for this design is always substantially the same thing—it is

always self-gratification in some form, and nothing else. We need to get this idea thoroughly into our minds. The general design of the sinner being always self-gratification, and it making very little if any difference in his guilt what form of self-gratification he chooses, it follows that the measure of guilt cannot be sought here, and must therefore be sought elsewhere.

8. But it is time I should state, positively, that guilt is always to be estimated by the degree of light under which the sinful intention is formed, or in other words, it is to be measured by the mind's knowledge or perception of the value of that end which the law requires to be chosen. This end is the highest well-being of God and of the universe. This is of infinite value ; and in some sense every moral agent must know it to be of infinite value, and yet individuals may differ indefinitely in respect to the degree of clearness with which this great end is apprehended by the mind. Choosing this end—the highest well-being of God and of the universe always implies the rejection of self-interest as an end ; and on the other hand, the choice of self-interest or self-gratification as an end always and necessarily implies the rejection of the highest well-being of God and of the universe as an end. The choice of either implies the rejection of its opposite.

Now the sinfulness of a selfish choice consists not merely in its choice of good to self, but in its implying a rejection of the highest well-being of God and of the universe as a supreme and ultimate end. If selfishness did not imply the apprehension and rejection of other and higher interests as an end, it would not imply

any guilt at all.  The value of the interests rejected is that
in which the guilt consists.  In others words the guilt
consists in rejecting the infinitely valuable well-being of
God and of the universe for the sake of selfish gratifi-
cation.

Now it is plain that the amount of guilt is as the
mind's apprehension of the value of the interests rejected.  In some sense, as I have said, every moral
agent has and must of necessity have the idea that the
interests of God and of the universe are of infinite
value.  He has this idea developed so clearly that every
sin he commits deserves endless punishment, and yet
the degree of his guilt may be greatly enhanced by
additional light, so that he may deserve punishment
not only endless in duration but indefinitely great in
degree.  Nor is there any contradiction in this.  If the
sinner cannot affirm that there is any limit to the value
of the interests he refuses to will and to pursue, he
cannot of course affirm that there is any limit to his
guilt and desert of punishment.  This is true and must
be true of every sin and of every sinner ; and yet as
light increases and the mind gains a clearer apprehension of the infinite value of the highest well-being of
God and of the universe, just in that proportion does
the guilt of sin increase.  Hence the measure of knowledge possessed of duty and its motives, is always and
unalterably the rule by which guilt is to be measured.

The proof of this is twofold.

1.  *The Scriptures assume and affirm it.*

The text affords a plain instance.  The apostle al-
ludes to those past ages when the heathen nations had

no written revelation of God, and remarks that "those times of ignorance God winked at". This does not mean that God connived at their sin because of their darkness, but does mean that he passed over it with comparatively slight notice, regarding it as sin of far less aggravation than those which men would now commit if they turned away when God commanded them all to repent. True, sin is never absolutely a light thing; but comparatively, some sins incur small guilt when compared with the great guilt of other sins. This is implied in our text.

I next cite James iv. 17. "To him that knoweth to do good, and doeth it not, to him it is sin." This plainly implies that knowledge is indispensable to moral obligation; and even more than this is implied; namely, that the guilt of any sinner is always equal to the amount of his knowledge on the subject. It always corresponds to the mind's perception of the value of the end which should have been chosen, but is rejected. If a man knows he ought in any given case to do good, and yet does not do it, to him this is sin—the sin plainly lying in the fact of not doing good when he knew he could do it, and being measured as to its guilt by the degree of that knowledge,

John ix. 41—"Jesus said unto them, if ye were blind, ye should have no sin: but now ye say, we see; therefore your sin remaineth". Here Christ asserts that men without knowledge would be without sin; and that men who have knowledge, and sin notwithstanding, are held guilty. This plainly affirms that the presence of light or knowledge is requisite to the existence of sin, and obviously implies that the amount of knowledge possessed is the measure of the guilt of sin.

It is remarkable that the Bible everywhere assumes first truths. It does not stop to prove them, or even assert them—it always assumes their truth, and seems to assume that every one knows and will admit them. As I have been recently writing on moral government and studying the Bible as to its teachings on this class of subjects, I have been often struck with this remarkable fact.

John xv. 22, 24—" If I had not come and spoken unto them, they had not had sin : but now they have no cloak for their sins. He that hateth me, hateth my Father also. If I had not done among them the works which none other man did, they had not had sin : but now have they both seen and hateth both me and my Father." Christ holds the same doctrine here as in the last passage cited—light essential to constitute sin, and the degree of light, constituting the measure of its aggravation. Let it be observed, however, that Christ probably did not mean to affirm in the absolute sense that if he had not come, the Jews would have had *no* sin ; for they would have had some light if he had not come. He speaks as I suppose comparatively. Their sin if he had not come would have been so much less as to justify his strong language.

Luke xii. 47, 48—" And that servant which knew his Lord's will, and prepared not himself, neither did according to his will, shall be beaten with many stripes. But he that knew not and did commit things worthy of stripes, shall be beaten with few stripes. For unto

whomsoever much is given, of him shall be much required ; and to whom men have committed much, of
him they will ask the more."

Here we have the doctrine laid down and the truth
assumed that men shall be punished according to
knowledge.   To whom much light is given, of him
shall much obedience be required.   This is precisely
the principle that God requires of men according to
the light  they have.

I Tim. i. 13—"Who was before a blasphemer, and
a persecutor, and injurious : but I obtained mercy, because I did it ignorantly in unbelief ".   Paul had done
things intrinsically as bad as well they could be ; yet
his guilt was far less because he did them under the
darkness of unbelief ; hence he obtained mercy, when
otherwise, he might not.   The plain assumption is
that his ignorance abated from the malignity of his
sin, and favoured his obtaining mercy.

In another passage (Acts xxvi. 9), Paul says of himself—" I verily thought with myself, that I ought to do
many things contrary to the name of Jesus of Nazareth ".   This had everything to do with the degree of
his guilt in rejecting the Messiah, and also with his
obtaining pardon.

Luke xxiii. 34—" Then said Jesus, Father, forgive
them ; for they know not what they do ".   This passage
presents to us the suffering Jesus, surrounded with
Roman soldiers and malicious scribes and priests, yet
pouring out his prayer for them, and making the only
plea in their behalf which could be made—" *for they
know not what they do* ".   This does not imply that

they had no guilt, for if that were true they would not have needed forgiveness ; but it did imply that their guilt was greatly palliated by their ignorance. If they had known him to be the Messiah, their guilt might have been unpardonable.

Matt. xi. 20-24—" Then began he to upbraid the cities wherein most of his mighty works were done, because they repented not. Woe unto thee, Chorazine ! woe unto thee, Bethsaida ! for if the mighty works which were done in you had been done in Tyre and Sidon, they would have repented long ago in sackcloth and ashes. But I say unto you it shall be more tolerable for Tyre and Sidon at the day of judgment than for you. And thou, Capernaum, which art exalted unto heaven, shalt be brought down to hell : for if the mighty works which have been done in thee, had been done in Sodom, it would have remained until this day. But I say unto you, that it shall be more tolerable for the land of Sodom, in the day of judgment, than for thee." But why does Christ thus upbraid these cities ? Why denounce so fearful a woe on Chorazin and Capernaum ? Because most of his mighty works had been wrought there. His oft-repeated miracles which proved him the Messiah had been wrought before their eyes. Among them he had taught daily, and in their synagogues every Sabbath day. They had great light ; hence their great—their unsurpassed guilt. Not even the men of Sodom had guilt to compare with theirs. The city most exalted, even as it were to heaven, must be brought down to the deepest hell. Guilt and punishment, evermore, according to light enjoyed but resisted.

Luke xi. 47-51—"Woe unto you! for ye build the sepulchres of the prophets, and your fathers killed them. Truly ye bear witness that ye allow the deeds of your fathers : for they indeed killed them, and ye build their sepulchres. Therefore also said the wisdom of God, I will send them prophets and apostles, and some of them they shall slay and persecute : that the blood of all the prophets, which was shed from the foundation of the world, may be required of this generation. From the blood of Abel, unto the blood of Zacharias, which perished between the altar and the temple : verily I say unto you, It shall be required of this generation." Now here, I ask, on what principle was it that all the blood of martyred prophets ever since the world began was required of that generation ? Because they deserved it ; for God does no such thing as injustice. It never was known that He punished any people or any individual beyond their desert.

But why and how did they deserve this fearful and augmented visitation of the wrath of God for past centuries of persecution ?

The answer is twofold : *they sinned against accumulated light : and they virtually endorsed all the persecuting deeds of their fathers*, and concurred most heartily in their guilt. They had all the oracles of God. The whole history of the nation lay in their hands. They knew the blameless and holy character of those prophets who had been martyred ; they could read the guilt of their persecutors and murderers. Yet under all this light, themselves go straight on and perpetrate deeds of the same sort, but of far deeper malignity.

Again, in doing this they virtually endorse all that their fathers did. Their conduct towards the Man of Nazareth, put into words would read thus—"The holy men whom God sent to teach and rebuke our fathers, they maliciously traduced and put to death; *they did right*, and we will do the same thing towards Christ". Now it was not possible for them to give a more decided sanction to the bloody deeds of their fathers. They underwrote for every crime—assume upon their own consciences all the guilt of their fathers. *In intention*, they do those deeds over again. They say, "If we had lived then we should have done and sanctioned all they did".

On the same principle the accumulated guilt of all the blood and miseries of Slavery since the world began rests on this nation now. The guilt involved in every pang, every tear, every blood-drop forced out by the knotted scourge—all lies at the door of this generation. Why? Because the history of all the past is before the pro-slavery men of this generation, and they endorse the whole by persisting in the practice of the same system and of the same wrongs. No generation before us ever had the light on the evils and the wrongs of Slavery that we have; hence our guilt exceeds that of any former generation of slave-holders; and, moreover, knowing all the cruel wrongs and miseries of the system from the history of the past, every persisting slave-holder endorses all the crimes and assumes all the guilt involved in the system and evolved out of it since the world began.

Rom. vii. 13—"Was then that which is good made

death unto me? God forbid. But sin, that it might appear sin, worketh death in me by that which is good, that sin by the commandment might become exceeding sinful." The last clause of this verse brings out clearly the principle that under the light which the commandment, that is, the law, affords, sin becomes exceedingly guilty. This is the very principle, which, we have seen, is so clearly taught and implied in numerous passages of Scripture.

The diligent reader of the Bible knows that these are only a part of the texts which teach the same doctrine: we need not adduce any more.

2. I remark that this is the rule and the only just rule by which the guilt of sin can be measured. If I had time to turn the subject over and over—time to take up every other conceivable supposition, I could show that none of them can possibly be true. No supposition can abide a close examination except this, that the rule or measure of guilt is the mind's knowledge pertaining to the value of the end to be chosen.

There can be no other criterion by which guilt can be measured. It is the value of the end chosen which constitutes sin guilty, and the mind's estimate of that value measures its own guilt. This is true according to the Bible as we have seen; and every man needs only consult his own consciousness faithfully and he will see that it is equally affirmed by the mind's own intuition to be right.

A few *inferences* may be drawn from our doctrine.

1. Guilt is not to be measured by the *nature* of the intention; for sinful intention is always a unit—always

one and the same thing—being nothing more nor less than self-gratification.

2. Nor can it be measured by the particular type of self-gratification which the mind may prefer. No matter which of his numerous appetites or propensities man may choose to indulge—whether for food, for strong drink—for power, pleasure, or gain—it is the same thing in the end—self-gratification, and nothing else. For the sake of this he sacrifices every other conflicting interest, and herein lies his guilt. Yet since he tramples on the greater good of others with equal recklessness, whatever type of self-gratification he prefers, it is plain that we cannot find in this type any true measure of his guilt.

3. Nor again is the guilt to be decided by the amount of evil which the sin may bring into the universe. An agent not enlightened may introduce great evil and yet no guilt attach to this agent. This is true of evil often done by brute animals. It is true of the mischiefs effected by alcohol. In fact it matters not how much or how little evil may result from the misdeeds of a moral agent, you cannot determine the amount of his guilt from this circumstance. God may overrule the greatest sin so that but little evil shall result from it, or he may leave its tendencies uncounteracted so that great evils shall result from the least sin. Who can tell how much or how little overruling agency may interpose between any sin great or small and its legitimate results?

Satan sinned in betraying Judas, and Judas sinned in betraying Christ. Yet God so overruled these sins that most blessed results to the universe followed from Christ's betrayal and consequent death. Shall the sins of Satan and Judas be estimated by the evils actually resulting from them? If it should appear that the good immensely overbalanced the evil, does their sin thereby become holiness—meritorious holiness? Is their guilt at all the less for God's wisdom and love in overruling it for good?

It is not therefore the amount of resulting good or evil which determines the amount of guilt, but is the degree of light enjoyed, under which the sin is committed.

4. Nor again can guilt be measured by the common opinions of men. Men associated in society are wont to form among themselves a sort of public sentiment which becomes a standard for estimating guilt; yet how often is it erroneous? Christ warns us against adopting this standard, and also against ever judging according to the outward appearance. Who does not know that the common opinions of men are exceedingly incorrect? It is indeed wonderful to see how far they diverge in all directions from the Bible standard.

5. The amount of guilt can be determined as I have said only by the degree in which those ideas are developed which throw light upon obligation. Just here sin lies, in resisting the light and acting in opposition to it, and therefore the degree of light should naturally measure the amount of guilt incurred.

### CONCLUSION

1. We see from this subject the principle on which many passages of Scripture are to be explained. It

might seem strange that Christ should charge the blood of all the martyred prophets of past ages on that· generation. But the subject before us reveals the principle upon which this is done and ought to be done.

Whatever of apparent mystery may attach to the fact declared in our text—" The times of this ignorance God winked at "—finds in our subject an adequate explanation. Does it seem strange that for ages God should pass over almost without apparent notice the monstrous and reeking abominations of the Heathen world? The reason is found in their ignorance. Therefore God winks at those odious and cruel idolatries. For all, taken together, are a trifle compared with the guilt of a single generation of enlightened men.

2. One sinner may be in such circumstances as to have more light and knowledge than the whole Heathen world. Alas! how little the Heathen know! How little compared with what is known by sinners in this land, even by very young sinners!

Let me call up and question some impenitent sinner of Oberlin. It matters but little who—let it be any Sabbath-school child.

What do you know about God?

I know that there is one God and only one.—The Heathen believe there are hundreds of thousands.

What do you know about this God?

I know that he is infinitely great and good.—But the Heathen thinks some of his gods are both mean and mischievous—wicked as can be and the very patrons of wickedness among men.

What do you know about salvation ?

I know that God so loved the world as to give his only begotten Son to die that whosoever would believe in him might live for ever. Oh! the heathen never heard of that. They would faint away methinks in amazement if they should hear and really believe the startling, glorious fact. And that Sabbath-school child knows that God gives his Spirit to convince of sin. He has perhaps often been sensible of the presence and power of that Spirit. But the Heathen know nothing of this.

You too know that you are immortal—that beyond death there is still a conscious unchanging state of existence, blissful or wretched according to the deeds done here. But the Heathen have no just ideas on this subject. It is to them as if all were a blank.

The amount of it then is that you know everything —the Heathen almost nothing. You know all you need to know to be saved, to be useful—to honour God and serve your generation according to his will. The Heathen sit in deep darkness, wedded to their abominations, groping, yet finding nothing.

As your light therefore, so is your guilt immeasurably greater than theirs. Be it so that their idolatries are monstrous—your guilt in your impenitence under the light you have is vastly more so. See that Heathen mother dragging her shrieking child and tumbling it into the Ganges ! See her rush with another to throw him into the burning arms of Moloch. Mark ;— see that pile of wood flashing, lifting up its lurid flames toward heaven. Those men are dragging a dead hus-

band—they heave his senseless corpse upon that burning pile. There comes the widow—her hair dishev-
eled and flying—gaily festooned for such a sacrifice;—
she dances on;—she rends the air with her howls and
her wailings;—she shrinks and yet she does not shrink
—she leaps on the pile, and the din of music with the
yell of spectators buries her shrieks of agony; she is
gone! Oh! my blood curdles and runs cold in my veins;
—my hair stands on end; I am horrified with such
scenes—but what shall we say of their guilt? Ah yes!
—what do they know of God—of worship—of the
claims of God ·upon their heart and life? Ah! you may
well spare your censure of the Heathen for their fearful orgies of cruelty and lust, and give it where light
has been enjoyed and resisted.

3. You see then that often a sinner in some of our
congregations may know more than all the Heathen
world know. If this be true, what follows from it as
to the amount of his comparative guilt? This inevit-
ably, *that such a sinner deserves a direr and deeper
damnation than all the Heathen world!* This conclusion may seem startling; but how can we escape from
it? We cannot escape. It is as plain as any mathematical demonstration. This is the principle asserted
by Christ when he said—" That servant which knew
his Lord's will and prepared not himself, neither did
according to his will, shall be beaten with many stripes;
but he that knew not and did commit things worthy
of stripes; shall be beaten with few stripes". How
solemn and how pungent the application of this doctrine would be in this congregation! I could call out

many a sinner in this place and show him that beyond question his guilt is greater than that of all the Heathen world. Yet how few ever estimated their own guilt thus.

Not long since an ungodly young man, trained in this country, wrote back from the Sandwich Islands a glowing and perhaps a just description of their horrible abominations, moralising on their monstrous enormities and thanking God that he had been born and taught in a Christian land. Indeed! he might well have spared this censure of the dark-minded Heathen. His own guilt in remaining an impenitent sinner under all the light of Christian America was greater than the whole aggregate guilt of all those Islands.

So we may all well spare our expressions of abhorrence at the guilty abominations of idolatry. You are often perhaps saying in your heart—Why does God endure these horrid abominations another day? See that rolling car of Juggernaut. Its wheels move axle deep in the gushing blood and crushed bones of its deluded worshippers! And yet God looks on and no red bolt leaps from its right hand to smite such wickedness. They are indeed guilty ; but Oh, how small their guilt compared with the guilt of those who know their duty perfectly, yet never do it! God sees their horrible abominations, yet does he wink at them because they are done in so much ignorance

But see that impenitent sinner. Convicted of his sin under the clear gospel light that shines all around him, he is driven to pray. He knows he ought to repent, and almost thinks he wants to, and will try. Yet

still he clings to his sins, and will not give up his heart
to God.   Still he holds his heart in a state of impenitence.   Now mark here;—his sin in thus withholding
his heart from God under so much light, involves
greater guilt than all the abominations of the heathen
world.   Put together the guilt of all those widows who
immolate themselves on the funeral pile—of those who
hurl their children into the Ganges, or into the burning
arms of Moloch—all does not begin to approach the
guilt of that convicted sinner's prayer who comes before God under the pressure of his conscience, and
prays a heartless prayer, determined all the while to
withhold his heart from God.   Oh! why does this sinner thus tempt God, and thus abuse his love, and thus
trample on his known authority?  Oh! that moment of
impenitence, while his prayers are forced by conscience
from his burning lips, and yet he will not yield the
controversy with his Maker—that moment involves
direr guilt than rests on all the Heathen world together!  He knows more than they all, yet sins despite of all his knowledge.   The many stripes belong
to him—the few to them.

4.   This leads me to remark again, that the Christian world may very well spare their revilings and con-
demnations of the Heathen.   Of all the portions of
earth's population, Christendom is infinitely the most
guilty— Christendom, where the gospels peals from ten
thousand pulpits—where its praises are sung by a
thousand choirs, but where many thousand hearts that
know God and duty, refuse either to reverence the one
or perform the other!   All the abominations of the

Heathen world are a mere trifle compared with the guilt of Christendom. We may look down upon the filth and meanness and degradation of a Heathen people, and feel a most polite disgust at the spectacle—and far be it from me, to excuse these degrading, filthy or cruel practices ; but how small their light, and consequently their guilt, compared with our own! We therefore ask the Christian world to turn away from the spectacle of Heathen degradation, and look nearer home, upon the spectacle of Christian guilt! Let us look upon ourselves.

5. Again, let us fear not to say what you must all see to be true, that the nominal church is the most guilty part of Christendom. It cannot for a moment be questioned, that the church has more light than any other portion; therefore has she more guilt. Of course I speak of the nominal church—not the real church whom he has pardoned and cleansed from her sins. But in the nominal church, think of the sins that live and riot in their corruption. See that backslider. He has tasted the waters of life. He has been greatly enlightened. Perhaps he has really known the Lord by true faith—and then see, he turns away to beg the husks of earthly pleasure! He turns his back on the bleeding Lamb! Now, put together all the guilt of every Heathen soul that has gone to hell—of every soul that has gone from a state of utter moral darkness, and your guilt, backsliding Christian, is greater than all theirs !

Do you, therefore, say—may God then, have mercy on my soul? So say we all ; but we must add if *it be possible;* for who can say that such guilt as yours can be forgiven! Can Christ pray for you as he prayed for his murderers—" Father, forgive them, for they know not what they do"? Can he plead in your behalf, that you knew not what you were doing? Awful! awful! Where is the sounding line that shall measure the ocean-depth of your guilt?

6. Again, if our children remain in sin, we may cease to congratulate ourselves that they were not born in Heathenism or slavery! How often have I done this! How often, as I have looked upon my sons and daughters, have I thanked God that they were not born to be thrown into the burning arms of a Moloch, or to be crushed under the wheels of Juggernaut! But if they will live in sin, we must suspend our self-congratulations for their having Christian light and privileges If they will not repent, it were infinitely better for them to have been born in the thickest Pagan darkness—better to have been thrown in their tender years into the Ganges, or into the fires which idolatry kindles—better be anything else, or suffer anything earthly, than have the gospel's light only to shut it out and go to hell despite of its admonitions.

Let us not, then, be hasty in congratulating ourselves, as if this great light enjoyed by us and by our children, were of course a certain good to them; but this we may do—we may rejoice that God will honour himself—his mercy if he can, and his justice if he must. God will be honoured, and we may glory in this. But Oh, the sinner, the sinner! Who can measure the depth of his guilt, or the terror of his final doom! It

will be more tolerable for all the Heathen world together than for you.

7. It is time that we all understood this subject
fully, and appreciated all its bearings. It is no doubt
true, that however moral our children may be, they are
more guilty than any other sinners under heaven, if
they live in sin, and will not yield to the light under
which they live. We may be perhaps congratulating
ourselves on their fair morality ; but if we saw their
case in all its real bearings, our souls would groan with
agony—our bowels would be all liquid with anguish—
our very hearts within us would heave as if volcanic
fires were kindled there—so deep a sense should we
have of their fearful guilt and of the awful doom they
incur in denying the Lord that bought them and setting at naught a known salvation. Oh ! if we ever pray,
we should pour out our prayers for our offspring as if
nothing could ever satisfy us or stay our importunity,
but the blessings of a full salvation realised in their
souls.

Let the mind contemplate the guilt of these children. I could not find a Sabbath-school child, perhaps not one in all Christendom who could not tell me
more of God's salvation than all the Heathen world
know. That dear little boy who comes from his Sabbath school knows all about the gospel. He is almost
ready to be converted, but not quite ready ; yet that
little boy, if he knows his duty and yet will not do it,
is covered with more guilt than all the Heathen
world together. Yes, that boy, who goes alone and
prays, yet holds back his heart from God, and then his

mother comes and prays over him, and pours her tears
on his head, and his little heart almost melts, and he
seems on the very point of giving up his whole heart
to the Saviour; yet if he will not do it, he commits
more sin in that refusal than all the sin of all the Heathen world—his guilt is more than the guilt of all the
murders, all the drownings of children, and burnings of
widows, and deeds of cruelty and violence in all the
Heathen world. All this combination of guilt shall
not be equal to the guilt of the lad who knows his
duty, but will not yield his heart to its righteous
claims.

8. "The Heathen," says an apostle, "sin without
law, and shall therefore perish without law." In their
final doom they will be cast away from God; this will
be perhaps about all. The bitter reflection, "I had
the light of the gospel and would not yield to it—I
knew all my duty, yet did it not"—this cannot be a
part of their eternal doom. This is reserved for those
who gather themselves into our sanctuaries and around
our family altars, yet will not serve their own Infinite
Father.

9. One more remark. Suppose I should call out a
sinner by name—one of the sinners of this congregation, a son of pious parents—and should call up the
father also, I might say, Is this your son? Yes.
What testimony can you bear about this son of yours?
I have endeavoured to teach him all the ways of the
Lord. Son, what can you say? I know my duty. I
have heard it a thousand times. I know I ought to
repent, but I never would.

Oh! if we understood this matter in all its bearings, it would fill every bosom with consternation and grief. How would our bowels burn and heave as a volcano! There would be one universal outcry of anguish and terror at the awful guilt and fearful doom of such a sinner!

Young man, are you going away this day in your sins? Then, what angel can compute your guilt? Oh! how long has Jesus held out his hands, yes, his bleeding hands, and besought you to look and live! A thousand times, and in countless varied ways has he called, but you have refused; stretched out his hands, and you have not regarded. Oh! why will you not repent? Why not say at once, It is enough that I have sinned so long! I cannot live so any longer! O sinner, *why will you live so?* Would you go down to hell—ah, to the deepest hell—where, if we would find you, we must work our way down a thousand years through ranks of lost spirits less guilty than you, ere we could reach the fearful depth to which you have sunk? O sinner, what a hell is that which can adequately punish such guilt as thine!

# 2

## THE SINNER"S DOOM

"He that, being often reproved, hardeneth his neck, shall suddenly be destroyed, and that without remedy."—*Proverbs* xxix. 1

IN discussing this subject I will consider :

    I. WHEN AND HOW PERSONS ARE REPROVED ;

    II. GOD'S DESIGN IN REPROVING SINNERS ;

    III. WHAT IT IS TO HARDEN THE NECK ;

    IV. WHAT IS INTENDED BY THE SINNER'S BEING
        SUDDENLY DESTROYED ; and

    V. WHAT IS IMPLIED IN ITS BEING WITHOUT
        REMEDY.

*I.* God's reproof of sinners may properly be considered as embracing three distinct departments ; namely, reproof by means of *his word*, by means of his *providence*, and through his *Spirit*. My limits will allow me to make only a few suggestions under each of these heads.

1. God reproves the sinner by his word whenever he in any way presents truth to his mind through his word, which shows the sinner his sins,—which reveals to him duties that he is not performing. Any such revelation of duties not done, and of sins positively committed, is reproof from God. Suppose you are a parent, and you point out to your child some neglect

of duty. You by this act reprove your child. There
may be connected with this some degree of threatening
explicitly announced, or there may not be ; in either
case it is reproof: for it must always be understood
that threatening is involved. Hence if you call the attention of your child to anything in his conduct which
displeases you, this very act is reproof. So when God
by the revealed truth of his word calls the sinner's attention to the fact of sin, he virtually reproves him,
and this is God's intention in calling his mind to the
fact of his sin.

2. By God's providence sinners are reproved, when
their selfish projects are defeated. Sinful men are continually planning selfish schemes, and God often through
his providence frustrates those schemes ; and does so for
the very purpose of reproving their projectors. He
could not rebuke them in a more emphatic way than
this.

Sinners often frame *ambitious* projects. The student
seeks for himself a great name as a scholar ; in other
spheres, men seek the renown of the warrior, or the
civilian—their aspiration being to enroll their names
high above their fellows on the pillar of fame ; but God
in his providence blasts their hopes, frustrates their
plans, and would fain make them see that they had better by far get their names written in the Lamb's book of
life. So he blots out their name on Ambition's scroll
as fast as they can write it there ;—as if he would show
them their folly, and allure them to write it where no
power can ever erase it.

Again, it often happens that men by means of their

selfishness become involved in difficulty ;—perhaps by
a selfish use of their property, or by a selfish indulgence
of their tongues ; and God springs his net upon them
and suddenly they are taken, and find themselves suddenly brought up to *think* of their ways, and to experience the mischiefs of their selfish schemes. How often
do we see this ! Men make haste to be rich, and start
some grasping scheme of selfishness for this purpose ;
but God suddenly springs his net upon them—blasts
their schemes, and sets them to thinking whether there
be not " a God in heaven who minds the affairs of
men ".

Another man finds himself entangled in lawsuits, and
his property melts away like an April snow ; and another pushes into some hazardous speculation—till the
frown of the Almighty rebukes his folly.

As men have a thousand ways to develop their selfishness, so God has a thousand ways to head them
back in their schemes and suggest forcibly to their
minds that " this their way is their folly ". In all such
cases men ought to regard themselves as taken in the
net of God's providence. God meets them in the narrow way of their selfishness, to talk with them about
the vanity and folly of their course.

Everything which is adapted to arrest the attention
of men in their sins may be regarded as a providential
reproof. Thus, when God comes among sinners and
cuts down some of their companions in iniquity, how
solemn often are those dispensations ! Often have I
had opportunity to notice these effects. Often have I
seen how solemn the minds of sinners become under

these reproofs of the Almighty. Their feelings become
tender ; their sensibilities to truth are strongly excited.
Who can fail to see that such events are designed to
arrest the attention, and to rebuke and reprove 'them in
their course of sin ?

Every obstacle which God in his providence inter-
poses in your way of selfishness, is *his* reproof. You
can regard it in no other light.

God sometimes reproves sinners in a way which may
be deemed more pungent than any other. I allude to
that way which the Bible describes as heaping coals of
fire on an enemy's head. A man abuses you ; and in
retaliation you do him all the good in your power.
Glorious retaliation ! How it pours the scorching lava
on his head ! Now God often does this very thing with
sinners. They sin against him most abusively and
most outrageously ;—and what does he do ? How
does he retaliate upon them ? Only by pouring out
upon them a yet richer flood of mercies ! He pours
new blessings into their lap till it runs over. He pros-
pers their efforts for property, enlarges their families
like a flock, and smiles on everything to which they put
their hand. Oh, how strangely do these mercies contrast
with the sinner's abuse of his great Benefactor !

I can recollect some cases of this sort in my own experience, when the deep consciousness of guilt made
me apprehend some great judgments from God. But
just then, God seemed in a most remarkable manner to
reveal his kindness and his love, and to show the great
meekness of his heart. Oh, what a rebuke of my sins
was this ! Could anything else so break my heart all to

pieces? Who does not know the power of kindness to melt the heart?

So God rebukes the sinner for his sins, and seeks to subdue his hard heart by manifested love.

Often sickness is to be regarded as a rebuke from God. When persons for selfish purposes abuse their health and God snatches it away, he in a most forcible way rebukes them for their madness.

Sometimes he brings the lives of men into great peril, so that there shall be but a step between them and death; —as if he would give this movement of his providence a voice of trumpet-power to forewarn them of their coming doom. So various and striking are the ways of God's providence in which he reproves men for their sins.

3. God also reproves men by his Spirit. According to our Saviour's teachings, the Spirit shall "reprove the world of sin, of righteousness, and of judgment". Hence when sinners are specially convicted of sin they should know that God has come in his own person to reprove them. His spirit comes to their very hearts, and makes impressions of truth and duty there—revealing to the sinner his own heart, and showing him how utterly at variance it is with a heart full of divine love.

Again, I have no doubt that in the present as in former days God reproves men of their sins by means of dreams. If all the reliable cases of this sort which have occurred since the Bible was completed were recorded, I doubt not they would fill many volumes. I am aware that some suppose this mode of divine operation upon the human mind has long ago ceased; but

I think otherwise. It may have ceased to be a medium of revealing new truth—doubtless it has ; but it has not ceased to be employed as a means of impressing and enforcing truth already revealed. Sometimes the great realities of the coming judgment and of the world of doom are brought out and impressed upon the mind with overwhelming force by means of dreams. When this is the case, who shall say that the hand of the Lord is not in it?

A striking instance of a dream in which the hand of the Lord may be seen, is related by President Edwards. One of his neighbours, an intemperate man, dreamed that he died and went to hell. I will not attempt to relate here the circumstances that according to his dream occurred there. Suffice it to say that he obtained permission to return to earth on probation for one year, and was told distinctly that if he did not reform within one year, he must come back again. Upon this he awaked, under most solemn impressions of the dreadful realities of the sinner's hell. That very morning he went to see his pastor, Pres. Edwards, who said to him —" This is a solemn warning from God to your soul. You must give heed to it and forsake your sins, or you are a ruined man for eternity." The man made very solemn promises. When he had retired, Edwards opened his journal and made an entry of the principal facts ;—the dream, the conversation, and of course the *date* of these events. The inebriate reformed and ran well for a time ; attended church and seemed serious ; but long before the year came round, he relapsed, returned to his cups, and ultimately in a fit of intoxica-

tion opened a chamber door in a shop which led down
an outside stairway—pitched headlong and broke his
neck.  Pres. Edwards turned to his journal and found
that the one year from the date of his dream came round
that very night, and the man's appointed time was up!

Now it is no doubt true that in general, dreams are
under the control of physical law, and follow, though
with much irregularity, the strain of our waking reve-
ries; and for this reason many persons will not believe
the hand of the Lord ever works in them; yet their
inference is by no means legitimate; for God certainly
*can* put his hand upon the mind dreaming as well as
upon the mind waking, and multitudes of instances in
point show that he sometimes does.

Again, God reproves the sinner whenever his Spirit
awakens in the mind a sense of the great danger of living in sin.  I have often known sinners greatly affected
with the thought of this danger—the terrible danger of
passing along through life in sin, exposed every hour to
an eternal and remediless hell.

Now these solemn impressions are God's kind warnings, impressed on the soul because he loves the sinner's well-being, and would fain save him if he wisely
can.

Often God's Spirit gives sinners a most impressive
view of the shortness of time.  He makes them feel
that this general truth applies in all its power *to themselves*—that their own time is short, and that they in
all probability have not long to live.  I am aware that
this impression sometimes originates in one's state of
health; but I also know that sometimes there is good

reason to recognise God's own special hand in it; and
that men sometimes ascribe to nervous depression of
spirits what should be ascribed directly to God himself.

Again, God often makes the impression that the present is the sinner's last opportunity to secure salvation.
I know not how many such cases have fallen under my
own observation, cases in which sinners have been made
to feel deeply that this is to be the very last offer of
mercy, and these the very last strivings of the Spirit.
My observation has taught me in such cases, to expect
that the result will verify the warning—that this is none
other than God's voice, and that God does not lie to
man, but teaches most solemn and impressive truth.
Oh, how does it become every sinner to listen and heed
such timely warnings!

Again, God's Spirit reproves sinners through their
particular friends, or through gospel ministers.  The
affectionate admonitions of a brother or a sister, a
parent or a child, a husband or a wife—how often have
these been the vehicle through which God has spoken
to the soul!  His ministers also, God often employs for
this purpose, so directing their minds that they in fact
present to the sinner the very truth which fits his case,
and he say, " It must be that somebody has told the
minister all about my thoughts and feelings.  Who can
it be?  I have never told anybody half so much of my
heart as he has preached to-day."  Now in such cases
you may be safe in ascribing the fitting truth to the
guiding hand of the divine Spirit.  God is making use
of his servant to reprove the sinner.

In all such cases as I have now been adducing, the reproofs administered should be ascribed to the Spirit of the Lord. In the same manner as God often in various ways administers consolation to penitent souls ; so does he administer reproof to the impenitent. He has a thousand modes of making his voice audible to the sinner's conscience, and in his wisdom he always selects such as he deems best adapted to produce the desired result.

*II. The design of God in reproving sinners.*

One thing aimed at is to press them with the means of reform. A benevolent God sincerely desires their salvation and honestly does all he wisely can to secure this desired result. Hence his oft-repeated reproofs and warnings. He will at least leave them without excuse. They shall never have it to say—" Oh, if we had only been forewarned of danger in those precious hours and years in which salvation was possible !" God designedly forestalls such exclamations by taking away all occasion, and putting in their mouths a very different one—" How have I hated instruction and my heart despised reproof ".

For this purpose God forewarns the sinner in season. Take the case of the man who dreamed of going down to hell. This dream was a loud and timely warning, adapted as well perhaps as any warning could be to induce reform and real repentance. It effectually took away all excuse or apology for persisting in his sins.

God designs by these reproofs to prepare men for the solemn judgment. It is in his heart to do them good —secure their seasonable—that is, their present, immediate repentance, so that they may meet their God in peace at last. His benevolence prompts him to this course and he pursues it with all his heart.

It is no doubt equally true that the great God designs to be ready himself for the final judgment—to meet every sinner there. He foresees that it will be important for him there to show how he has dealt with each sinner—how often and how faithfully he has acted towards them the part of a kind Father. For this end every reproof ever given to a sinner will come in place. That dream recorded by Pres. Edwards will then be found recorded also by an angel's pen—to be revealed before all worlds then and there! This is one step in the process of parental efforts for reclaiming one sinner. The admonition so faithfully given by Pres. Edwards is another. All will go to show that truly God has been " long suffering towards sinners because he is not willing that any should perish, but that all should come to repentance ".

Thus will God in these providential warnings glorify Himself by exhibiting his true character and conduct. Nothing more is ever needful in order to glorify God than that his true character and conduct should be known as it is. The developments brought out at the judgment-day will thus reveal God, and of course will enhance his glory.

It is also interesting to see how God makes one warning create another. One providential event, sent as a judgment upon one sinner, multiplies its warning voice many fold as it falls upon the ears of hosts of other sinners. God cuts down one out of a class of hoary sinners, or of sinners in middle life, or in youth, and the event speaks in notes of solemn warning to hundreds. At Rome, N. Y., several years ago a great revival occurred, the power of which rocked and rent the stout hearts of many sinners, as the forest trees are rocked and rent by a tornado; but with it came some awful judgments revealing another form of the mighty hand of God. There were in that place a small class of hard drinkers who seemed determined to resist every call from God to repent. On the Sabbaths they would get together for drinking and revelling. On one of these occasions, one of their number suddenly fell down dead. Mr. Gillett, pastor of the church in that place, hastened to the spot, found the fallen man yet warm, but actually dead; and turning to the surrounding company of his associates, said "There— who of you can doubt that this man has gone right down to hell!" This case made a deep and thrilling impression.

Another man, a famous apostate from a profession of religion, greatly opposed the revival. All at once God smote him with madness, and in his insane ravings he sought to take his own life. Men by turns had to watch him and restrain him by violence from committing suicide. Ere long he died a most horrid death—an awful warning to hardened apostates of their impending doom! So God tries to reform and save guilty men.

Again, God would manifest the utter madness, recklessness, and folly of sinners. How striking it will appear in the judgment to see such a multitude of cases of reproof brought out to light, and then in connection to see the folly and madness of sinners in resisting so

many reproofs! What a gazing-stock will sinners then
be to the gathered myriads of intelligent beings! I
have sometimes thought this will be the greatest wonder of the universe, to see the men who have displayed
such perfect and long-continued infatuation in resisting
so much love and so many kind and most heart-affect-
ing appeals and reproofs! There they will stand mon-
uments of the voluntary infatuation of a self-willed
sinner! The intelligent universe will gaze at them as
if they were the embodiment of all that is wondrous in
madness and folly!

*III. What is it to harden the neck?*

The figure is taken from the effect of the yoke on the
bullock. Under constant pressure and friction the skin
becomes callous, and past feeling. So with the sinner's
conscience. His will has resisted truth until his constant opposition has hardened his moral sensibility, and
his will rests in the attitude of rebellion against God.
His mind is now fixed; reproofs which have heretofore
chafed his sensibilities no longer reach them; friction
and resistance have hardened his heart till he is past
feeling. No dispensations of providence alarm him:
no voice from God disturbs him; under all appeals to his
reason or conscience his will is doggedly fixed; his
moral feelings are insensible.

In this state, one might well say, the neck is hardened. The figure is pertinent. Who has not seen
cases of this sort? cases of men who have become so
hardened that every reproof passes by them as if it
touched them not—as if their moral sensibility had
ceased to be any sensibility at all. I was struck the

other day in conversing with a man of seventy-five, with his apparent insensibility to religious considerations. "Are you a Christian?" said I. "No; I don't know anything about them things—what you call Christians. I never murdered anybody, and I guess I have been as honest as most folks in my way." "But are you prepared to enter heaven—to go into another state of existence, and meet God face to face?" "Oh! I don't believe anything about them things. If I only live about right, that's enough for me." I could make no impression on such a mind as his; but God will make such men know something about these things by and by. They will change their tone ere long!

You sometimes see men in this condition who have given their intelligence up to embrace error, and have of free choice put darkness for light, and light for darkness; have stultified themselves in their own iniquities, and have said to evil, "Be thou my good". These have a scared conscience and a hard heart; their neck is an iron sinew, and they are fixed and fully set never to yield to God's most reasonable demands.

What, then, shall God do with such men? The text tells us. They "shall be suddenly destroyed, and that without remedy". This leads me to inquire:

*IV. What is meant by being suddenly destroyed?*

It implies their being cut off *unexpectedly*, in such an hour as they think not. We often speak of things as coming suddenly; not because they come early in life, but because they fall upon men all suddenly and without being at all anticipated. In this sense the term *suddenly* seems to be used in our text. When some awful stroke of God's providence falls suddenly among us, smiting down some sinner in his sins, we say—What a sudden death! what an awful dispensation! So the Bible says, while they cry " Peace and safety, then sudden destruction cometh upon them, and they shall not escape ". No forewarning is given ; no herald with trumpet-call proclaims the coming of that death-shaft ; but all suddenly it cuts the air and strikes its blow! It has no need to strike another! Noiseless as the falling dew it comes ; with velvet step it enters his bed-chamber ; in such forms as no skill or power of man can baffle, it makes its approaches ; death raises his bony arm—poises that never-erring shaft—in a moment, *where is the victim ?* Gone ; but *where ?* The Bible says, he is " suddenly destroyed ". Does this mean that he is borne up as on a chariot of fire to heaven ? Were the wicked men of Sodom and Gomorrah—" set forth as an ensample " of the doom of the wicked— caught away up to heaven in mounting columns of fire and brimstone? If that had been, methinks all heaven would have fainted at the sight! Or were the people of the old world, who had all corrupted their way before God, and who were so full of violence and bloodshed that God could not endure them on earth—were they all swept by the flood into heaven, while poor Noah, scorned by the men of his generation, must toil many long years to prepare him an ark to save himself and family from being also *destroyed into heaven ?*

What infinite trifling is this with God's words, to say that the sinner's destruction is only taking him by the shortest route and the quickest inway to heaven !

Does God say or mean this? No! If it had been his purpose to deceive men, he could not have taken a more direct and certain method than this, of calling the taking of men suddenly to heaven, *destruction!* No, this mode of using language belongs to Satan and not to God! We should never confound the broad distinction between the God of truth and the Father of lies!

*V. What is meant when this destruction is said to be " without remedy " ?*

1. That this destruction cannot be arrested. It comes with resistless and overwhelming power, and seems to mock all efforts made to withstand its progress. A most striking exemplification of this appeared in the dreadful *Cholera* which swept over many of our cities some years ago. I was then in New York city—an eye-witness and more than an eye-witness of its terrific power. My own system experienced its withering shock. A man of the strongest constitution occupied a room adjacent to mine; was attacked the same hour that I was, and within a few hours was a corpse. Its powerful sweep was appalling. You might as well put forth your hand to stay the tornado in its rush of power as think to withstand this messenger of the Almighty. So with those forms of destruction which come at God's behest to whelm the hardened sinner in destruction. They come with the strides and the momentum of Omnipotence. The awful hand of God is in them, and who can stand before him when once his wrath is moved?

Many other forms of disease, as well as the Cholera, evince the terror of Jehovah's arm. The strong man is bowed low; his physician sits by his bed-side, power-less to help; disease mocks all efforts to withstand its progress; human skill can only sit by and chronicle its triumph. God is working, and none but a God could resist.

2. The very language shows that the principal idea of the writer is that this destruction is *endless*. It is *destruction*—the utter ruin of all good—the blighting and withering of all happiness for ever. No rescue shall be possible; recovery is hopeless; it is a grave beyond which dawns no resurrection. The destruction wrecks all hope in the common ruin, and in its very terms precludes the idea of remedy. Can you conceive of another element of terror, not already involved and developed in this most dire of all forms of destruction?

## CONCLUSION

1. We see how to account for the sudden deaths of the wicked that occur often, and what we are to think of them. Some such deaths have occurred here which were exceedingly striking to me. Here we have seen young men, sons of pious parents, children of many prayers and many warnings; but they waxed hard under reproof; and their days were soon numbered. Away they go—and we see them no more. There was one young man who came here to study. He had been warned and prayed for. Perhaps the Lord saw that there was no hope in any further effort. His sickness I can never forget; nor his horror as death drew on apace. Away he passed from the world of hope and mercy. I will not attempt to follow him, nor would I

presume to know his final doom ;—but one thing I know ; —his companions in sin received in his death a most solemn and awful warning.

2. The danger of wicked men is in proportion to the light they have. Men of great light are much the most likely to be cut off in early life. Of this we have seen some very striking instances in this place. Some young men have been raised here—were here when I came into the place, and then, in the tender years of child- hood and youth they saw their companions converted, and were often affectionately warned themselves. But they seemed to resist every warning and come quick to maturity in moral insensibility. I need not give their names: you knew them once; where are they now? It is not for me to tell where they are ;—but I can tell where they are not. They are not grown up to bless the church and the world ; they did not choose such a course and such an end to their life. They are not here among us. No! the places that knew them once shall know them no more for ever. You may call for them in our College halls; in the sad-hearted families where once they might be found ;—they respond to no call—till the blast of the final trumpet. They knew their duty but too well, and but too soon they apparently settled the question that they *would not do it.*

That old man of almost fourscore of whom I spake was not brought up in any Oberlin. His birthplace was in the dark places of the earth—in Canada—where he learned neither to read nor to write. There are chil- dren here not ten years old who have forty times as much knowledge on all religious subjects as he. He has lived to become hoary in sin ; these children, brought up here, need expect no such thing. Tell me where you can find an old man who has been brought up in the midst of great light, who yet lives long and waxes more and more hard in sin and guilt. Usually such men as sin against great light in their youth will not live out half their days.

3. It is benevolent in God to make his providential judgments in cutting down hardened sinners a means of warning others. Often this is the most impressive warning God can give men. In some cases it is so terrible that sinners have not even dared to attend the funeral of their smitten associates. They have seemed afraid to go near the awful scene—so manifest has it been that God's hand is there. In many instances within my personal knowledge the hand of God has cut down in a most horrible manner men who were opposing revivals. I cannot now dwell upon these cases.

4. We may learn to expect the terrible destruction of those who under great light are hardening themselves in sin. I have learned, when I see persons passing through great trials, to keep my eye on them and see if they reform. If they do not, I expect to see them ere long cut down as hopeless cumberers of the ground. Being often reproved yet still hardening their neck, they speedily meet their doom according to the principle of God's government announced in our text.

5. Reproof administered either soon subdues, or rapidly ripens for destruction. This ripening process goes on rapidly in proportion to the pressure with which

God follows them with frequent and solemn reproofs. When you see God following the sinner close with frequent reproofs, plying him with one dispensation after another, and all in vain, you may expect the lifted bolt to smite him next and speedily.

6. The nearer destruction is to men, the less as a general thing they fear or expect it. When you hear them cry "Peace and safety," then sudden destruction is at hand and they shall not escape. Just at the time when you are saying—"I never enjoyed better health"—just then when you are blessing yourself in the prospect of securing your favourite objects, then sudden destruction comes down like an Alpine avalanche, and there is neither time to escape nor strength to resist. How often do you hear it said—Alas! it was so unexpected, so sudden—who would have thought this blow was coming! Just when we least of all expected it, it fell with fatal power.

7. Sinners who live under great light are living very fast. Those who are rapidly acquiring knowledge of duty, standing in a focal centre of blazing light, with everything to arouse their attention—they, unless they yield to this light, must soon live out the short months of their probation. They must soon be converted, or soon pass the point of hope—the point within which it is morally possible that they shall be renewed. Men may under some circumstances live to the age of seventy and never get so much light as they can in a few days or weeks in some situations. Under one set of circumstances a sinner might get more light, commit more sin, and become more hardened in a twelvemonth

than he would under other circumstances in a life of fourscore years. Under the former circumstances he lives fast. A Sabbath-school child might in this point of view die a hundred years old. The accumulations of a hundred years of sin and guilt and hardness might in his case be made in one short year. Where light is blazing as it has blazed here; where children have line upon line as they are wont to have here, how rapidly they live! How soon do they fill up the allotted years of probation for the reason that the great business of probation is driven through with prodigiously accelerated rapidity! Oh, how suddenly will your destruction come, unless you speedily repent! Of all places on earth, this should be the last to be chosen to live in, unless you mean to repent. I would as soon go to the very door of hell and pitch my tent to dwell there, as to come here to live, unless I purposed to serve God. Yet many parents bring or send their children here to be educated—in hope often that they will be converted too; and this is well; so would I; but by all means ply them with truth, and press them with appeals and entreaties, and give them no rest, till they embrace the great salvation. Let these parents see to it that their children are really converted. If they pass along without being converted, do you not expect they will soon break away and plunge into some of the dark mazes of error? Who does not know that this is the natural result of resisting great light? "Because they receive not the love of the truth that they may be saved, God shall send them strong delusion, that they may believe a lie, and all be dammed who believed not the truth but had pleasure in unrighteousness." Oh how they go on with rapid strides down to the depths of hell! You scarce can say they are here, before they are gone. And the knell of their early graves proclaims, " He that, being often reproved, hardeneth his neck, shall suddenly be destroyed, and that without remedy ".

# 3

## WHEN A SOUL IS LOST

"For what shall it profit a man if he shall gain the whole world and lose his own soul? Or what shall a man give in exchange for his soul?"—Mark viii. 36, 37

OURS is an inquisitive world, and the present especially is an inquisitive age. Particularly is this inquisitiveness developed in perpetual inquiries upon matters of loss and gain. Almost universally this class of questions agitates the public mind, often tasking its powers to the utmost. Almost the whole race seem all on fire to know how they can avoid loss and secure gain. Assuredly therefore, this being the great question which men interest themselves to ask, it cannot be out of place for God to propose such a question as the text presents, nor for his servants to take it from his lips and press it upon the attention and the consciences of his hearers.

And let me here say, it must be specially proper to propose it to the young men who are seeking good, and studying questions of profit and gain. Your souls thirst for happiness. How much, then, does it become you to ask whether these questions from the lips of your Redeemer may not give you a priceless clue to the secret of all real and permanent good.

The question concisely expressed is, *What is a*

*fair equivalent for the soul? For what consideration could a man afford to lose his soul?*

To bring the subject fully before your minds, let me

I.  DIRECT YOUR ATTENTION TO THE WORTH OF THE SOUL;

II.  TO THE DANGER OF LOSING IT;

III.  TO THE CONDITIONS OF SAVING IT.

*I.* Whenever ministers enter the pulpit to preach, they always take many things for granted. All do this more or less; all must do it if they would preach with any effectiveness to the heart; and it is right that they should. This is true not of the gospel minister only, but of every teacher. Every teacher assumes that his pupils exist, and that they know this truth; also, that he exists himself.

Many other truths are assumed by the preacher. We must always begin somewhere. Generally we begin as the Bible does. The Bible assumes the truths of natural theology, and proceeds in its teachings as if all men knew at least these truths.

This congregation professes to be Christian, and I may therefore assume that at least nominally it is so. I shall not therefore address you as a heathen people, or as atheists, or even Universalists.

There are certain great truths admitted by almost all Christians; for example, *that the soul is immortal.* This is admitted so generally, I shall assume that you all admit it. You admit it to be true of both the righteous and the wicked. You admit that the Bible teaches this, and I shall not therefore attempt to prove it.

It must also be admitted that, from the very nature of mind, its capacities, both of intellect and sensibility, will be always increasing. This increase is obviously a law of mind in this world, although, from the connection of mind with matter, old age and disease seem to form an exception. This is indeed an exception to the common law, yet one which plainly results from the influence of physical frailty, and can therefore have no existence in a state where no physical frailty is experienced. It must be admitted that the exception does not result from any law of mind, but purely from a present law of matter.

The common law of mental progress is exceedingly apparent. Put your eye on the new-born infant. It knows nothing. It begins with the slightest perception, it may be of some visible object, or of the taste of its food. From a starting-point almost imperceptible it goes on, making its hourly accessions of knowledge and consequent expansion of powers, till, like a Newton, it can fathom the sublime problem of the great law of the physical universe.

It is generally admitted that the capacities of men in the future state for either happiness or misery will be full—absolutely *full*. That coming state must be in respect to enjoyment, not mixed like the present, but simple ;—unalloyed bliss, or unalleviated woe. Hence the soul must actually enjoy or suffer to the uttermost limit of its capacity. You all admit this ; or if not all, the exceptions are few and I am not aware of any among you.

Let us not forget to connect with this idea of progression the idea of eternity. It is not only progress, but *eternal* progress. This is involved in the immortality of the soul. No doctrine is more plainly taught and more universally implied in the Bible; none is more amply confirmed by testimony drawn from the nature of the soul itself. It stands among the truths admitted by almost every one who bears even nominally the Christian name.

Now what follows from these admitted truths?

If men are always to progress in knowledge and capacity, then a period will arrive in which the least intelligence will be able to say, I know more now than all the created universe knew when I was born. This must be true. Its truth follows by necessity from the truths we have admitted.

But even this is not all. For when he has reached this point of acquisition in knowledge, he has only begun. Eternity is yet before him. The time will come when he will know ten thousand times as much as all the universe did when he was born; nay, not merely ten thousand times as much, but myriads of myriads of times as much. The time will arrive in the lapse of eternal ages when, if all the present created universe were tasked to the utmost to conceive or estimate how much this one intelligence can know, they would fall entirely short of reaching the mighty conception. And even this is only a mere beginning, for this vast intelligence is not a whit nearer the terminus of his progression than when he was one day old. To be sure, all the universe have kept pace with him. They have all moved along together, under a law of progress

common to them all. Each one can say the same and
as much as he. The attainments of each and of all
will for ever fall short of infinite, although they are
always indefinitely increasing.

Look at the happiness of the righteous. Always
increasing ; ever more swelling its deep and gushing
tides, with no limit to their growth and no end to their
progression. Who does not know that this must be so ?
Look at the little infant. It seems to have but the
least possible capacity, and this is developed at first
only in its physical powers. All the earliest germs of
sensation and emotion pertain to the body alone. The
little one is hungry and cries ; then is nursed and is
quiet ; it opens its little eye and beholds the light and
is pleased ; by-and-by it comes to know its mother's
presence, and to love that beaming look of fondness
and those soothing tones of love. Here opens to that
infant mind a new source of happiness, and new powers
begin to develop themselves. The little one smiles re-
sponsive to the smiles of its now known mother, and
enjoys the pleasure of being caressed and loved. Then
on and on through opening life : new knowledge opens
new sources of happiness ; progress—progress is the
established law of our mental and sentient being. By-
and-by that child, late an infant, is a pupil in school,
and then a youth in college. On and still onward is
his progress in knowledge.

Nor let us lose sight of the fact that the same law of
progress obtains also in the department of the sensibility. A uniform relation is maintained between man's
intellectual and sentient faculties. Knowledge increas-

ing gives scope for increased joys or sorrows. Thus
the mind progresses through all the stages of its earthly
existence, new knowledge continually opening new
sources of enjoyment or suffering. Mark how much
that man or woman is capable of enjoying, compared
with the capacity of his or her period of infancy. Now
he may be bowed down under an overwhelming weight
of sorrow, or he may be lifted up in ecstasies of joy
unspeakable and full of glory. And this progress, we
should remark, is often made despite of very unfavour-
able circumstances. The law of progress acts with a
positive energy that no ordinary circumstances can resist.

But let us now look into the next world—the next
state of our existence. Knowledge sustains still the
same relation to the sensibility ; what you know there
serves no less than it did here to augment your bliss or
aggravate your woe. All the powers of your being
sustain the same mutual relation as ever. Just think
then how vast the joys and sorrows of that coming
state ! Mark how they tower high above all that is
ever experienced in this brief state ! This is no poetry.
It is more than poetry—infinitely more ! It is too
obviously and certainly true to admit of the least question. Its truth results from admissions you make and
doctrines you hold as a Christian congregation—admissions and doctrines common to all who are not atheists
—common to all who observe the laws of our present
existence and who admit that these laws will follow
our existence into our future state of being.

Following out these admitted truths to their necessary
results, we see that the time must come, in the lapse of

eternal ages, when each saint can say, I now enjoy
more in a given time than all the saints in the universe
did when I first entered heaven.  For, as with knowledge, so with happiness : it must of course come under
the same law of progress.  Its measure must sustain
its established correlation to the amount of our knowledge ; so that, as the one stretches onward and still
onward, with no limit to its progress, so also does the
other.  As therefore the time will come when no created
mind can estimate the knowledge attained by the
now feeblest intelligence, so will it also come when no
capacity can estimate the measure of its happiness.
The Bible say, God is able to do exceeding abundantly
above all we are able to ask or even to think.  This
will have its striking fulfilment in the future heights of
bliss and glory to which he will raise his redeemed
people.  Oh, who can measure these heights of bliss
and glory !  Yet when you have fixed your eye upon
their towering loftiness at any period along the track of
endless ages, you have it to say then and there, This
man's happiness is only begun.  He has only just
entered upon his everlasting progress in knowledge and
in bliss.  And still, so vast are his capacities at this
remote period of his existence, that, if we could look
into their amazing length and breadth and depth, and
measure their magnitude, we should sink like dead men
at the sight.  See him drawing draughts of joy from
God's own eternal fountains.  Will he ever cease to
quaff those draughts of joy ?  Never.  Can they ever
grow less ?  Nay ; they must of necessity be for ever
increasing.

Now see also the progress of the wicked. They, too, are moving onward. The law of progress cannot be arrested by any amount of sinning. Onward still their minds are progressing : more and more capacious for knowledge, and of course for sin and suffering. And Oh! What then? What follows from these established laws of the human mind and of human existence? Let your reflections trace out the fearful results which accrue from these laws of eternal progression. When we get into the midst of these things, the mind becomes exhausted and overpowered; it sinks down and cries out with crushing emotion, Oh! what an eternity is this for the sinner, lost for ever! Oh! look upon that sinner after he has passed along through millions of ages of his unceasing progress in knowledge and in growing capacities for sin and suffering. Hear him. He says, Hell knew but little of sin and suffering when I came here compared with what I suffer now! They all then sinned and suffered but little, even taken in the vast aggregate, compared with what I sin and suffer in my own single being now! Alas, I seem to have all hell in my own bosom! I sin and suffer enough with my vastly augmented powers to make an awful hell even if these agonies were equally distributed among myriads of my fellow-beings. How awful! Sin, misery, and ruin enough to make one awful hell, locked up in the agonised bosom of a single sinner!

If this were only poetry I should be glad, but all is true, and so much more is true that no language can express it; no modes of computation and no forms of estimate can reach its appalling magnitude. So much

is true that to see the thousandth part of it must set
your soul all on fire!

Take any sinner here—any young man or woman
from this congregation. Follow him onward from this
hour through a life of sinning, a death of darkness and
horror, and then onward still as he rolls in the agonies
of the second death, and moves onward, age after age
in the unceasing progress of a human mind expanding
its intelligence, learning more and more of the God the
sinner hates, and only hating Him for ever the more,
and only making himself the more immeasurably
wretched by sinning with more bitter hate, and suffering with still enlarged capacities as the eternal years
roll on! O young man! you will one day be able to
say, All that hell knew of suffering before I came here
is nothing compared with what I now suffer. All is
nothing to the aggregate of my sins and of my sufferings. And all I now endure is only a beginning. My
miseries have only begun. This soul of mine has only
begun to know how to suffer the real sufferings of the
damned. Its keen sensitiveness to agony has only
begun to develop itself. Yet at some period in the flow
of those endless years of progression in sorrow, each
one will say, If all the universe at the moment of my
death had taxed their minds to the utmost to conceive the guilt and miseries that wring my heart,
they could not even have begun to reach the appalling
estimate!

Would to God this were only poetry! Alas, that it
should be among the best established truths in the
universe of realities! Young man, there is no axiom

in mathematics more true than this. No problem you ever solved in algebra brought out its result with more certainty ; no proposition of Euclid ever carried you more unerringly to its conclusions, than our reasoning upon these known and changeless laws of mind in their progression onward through the endless cycles of eternity. Go onward and still onward ; you must yet say, after ever so many periods of largest conception, I have only just begun. I am only entering the vestibule of this world of woe—only counting off the first moments, as it were, of the eternal cycles of my existence !

To pursue this train of thought in its details seems utterly impossible ! How the mind sinks beneath the overpowering view ! Oh, the worth of the soul, progressing for ever under a law as fixed as, and as enduring as, Jehovah's throne ! The worth of a soul that must make progress in knowledge, and consequently in its capacities for bliss and for holiness, or for sin and for woe—who can estimate it to the last fraction ! Tell me, ye young men of mathematical genius—ye professors in this science of certainties—ye who think ye have some knowledge of fixed truths and some skill in educing them from first principles ; tell me, are these things poetry ? You know they are eternal truth ; you know they are verities, than which none in the universe can be more sure. " What, then, shall it profit a man, if he shall gain the whole world, and lose his own soul ? "

*II.* But what must be said of the *danger of losing the soul !*

This danger is exceedingly great, because men have

only to neglect the soul and it is surely lost. It does not require attention and labour. You can lose your soul without the least possible effort made specially for this purpose. You need not go about to commit sin in order to insure the ruin of your soul hopelessly and for ever. You need only neglect its salvation and it is surely lost. You need only be as negligent as you have been heretofore. It is only necessary that you slide along in the same thoughtless, reckless manner as in your past days, and the end will be " sudden destruction, and that without remedy ". As says the Apostle : "How shall we escape, if we neglect so great salvation?" There is none other name under heaven given among men whereby ye can be saved. And there is no salvation through this name but by a living faith which works by love and makes the heart pure from sin.

Men will lose their souls *if they mistake the conditions of salvation.* For these conditions require intelligent effort, and to misunderstand them makes it certain that your efforts will not be made intelligently, even if any sort of effort is made at all. There is, therefore, most imminent danger in this quarter.

Again, there is the more danger because men are so little inclined to inform themselves respecting those truths which relate to the conditions of salvation. It is a most astounding fact that, in matters so deeply interesting to every one who is to be saved or lost, no man should incline to search after the requisite knowledge of the way to be saved.

There is also the more danger because men are surrounded with temptations to neglect the soul's salvation.

It is the policy of Satan to surround men with as many temptations as possible to neglect this great subject. He gives them everything else to do; sets their wits at work to kill time and devise amusing and diverting occupations, and stave off all serious thought into some unknown future. Nothing delights or employs him more than to draw the sinner in and hold him fast in the snare of his infernal devices.

Again, there is the more ground to fear because you are in so much danger of practising deception upon yourself, especially this deception,—that you can better attend to the saving of your soul at some other time. This is Satan's masterpiece of deception. It has fixed the doom of damnation upon myriads of souls.

If I had time to enter upon these various dangers and expand them at length in view of the awfulness of losing the soul, how startling would be the fearful facts of the case! If all these countless dangers were seen in their real magnitude, and especially if they were seen in their bearings upon the loss of a soul, methinks it would rouse all mankind into excitement almost to madness in securing the salvation of their souls. How could they refrain from crying out in the very streets, and within the very walls of their bedchambers, What shall I do to be saved from such a hell? The danger is real, although due sensibility to it is so rare. We have it from the lips of one that knew—" Broad is the way that leadeth to destruction, and many there be that go in thereat". And no fact is more open to observation than this. Everybody sees it; all may know it.

*III.   What are the conditions of saving the soul ?*

Here let it be well considered that the conditions are
none of them arbitrary.   All are naturally necessary.
Each one is revealed as a condition, because, in the nature of the case, it is and must be.   God requires it as a
condition because he cannot save the soul without it.
For example, you must be sanctified and become holy
in heart and life.   Why?   Not because God sees fit
arbitrarily to impose such a condition, but because it is
impossible you should be happy without it ; because it
is impossible you should enjoy heaven, and therefore
inadmissible that you should enter heaven, without
holiness.

So, also, you must be sanctified by faith in Christ, and
saved in all respects by this faith, for the simple reason
that no other agency can sanctify and save.   There is
none other name given among men whereby ye can be
saved.   No other Redeemer exists to be believed in ;
no other power but that of faith in such a Redeemer
ever yet reached the heart to subdue it to submission,
penitence, and love.

### CONCLUSION

1.   There is nothing more wonderful and strange
than the tendency of the human mind to neglect reflection and serious thought upon the value of the soul.
The entire orthodox world admit the truths upon which
we started, and admit substantially those other truths
which are necessarily connected with them.   Now it is
most astounding that these truths should be dropped
out of mind—their bearings forgotten, and all their

relations be overlooked as if they had no value, as if they were indeed only fictions and not facts. They are forgotten by parents, so that few indeed think of the bearings of these truths upon their children's well-being for eternity ; they are forgotten by husbands and by wives, so that in these relations of life little is said, little felt, little done, for each other's salvation. In fact, these great truths have come to be less regarded than almost any one of the ten thousand things of this world. The least of these worldly matters is practically treated as of more value than the soul. Must there not be a strange delirium upon the human mind ?

2.  Nothing is so important to the Christian church and to the world as that the church should direct her attention to these great things till they arouse her whole soul !—till they awaken from spiritual lethargy every member of Christ's nominal church on earth. The Primitive Christians of apostolic times pondered these truths until their hearts were on fire, and they could not wish to do less than to lay themselves out for the salvation of the world. The same engrossing and soul-stirring attention to these great truths is needed to awaken the churches of the present day.

3.  As these great truths of the soul are neglected, worldly things magnify themselves in apparent importance. If men do not dwell upon eternity, time comes to be their only reality. If they do not dwell upon the great spiritual truths that relate to the eternal world, to heaven and to hell ; if they do not pour their minds out upon these truths, the trifles of time will assume the chief importance. Men will become worldly-minded.

Their minds become contracted, in the scope of their views, to the narrow circle of their earthly relations, and they come to live as if there were no God, no heaven, no hell.

4. You may see the nature of worldly-mindedness. It is real *insanity*. Suppose a man to act as if he had no relations to this world. Suppose he should act as if he had no more to do with it than most men seem to have with the other world beyond this. Let him act as if he had no bodily wants—no occasion for food or for clothing. Of course he would be regarded as a madman; his friends, or, if not they, the civil authorities, would hasten to put him in a madhouse. They would sue out a commission of lunacy against him, to save his property, if he had any, for the benefit of himself and his family. For precisely this is real insanity—overlooking real facts and acting as if they did not exist.

But what shall we say of those who treat these truths of eternity as if they were not truths? Is not this also real insanity? The man *knows* the great facts respecting the future world. He has a book well authenticated, containing all the facts, fully revealed; he holds all the important facts with the utmost tenacity, and would deem himself slandered as a heretic if you were to intimate a doubt of the soundness of his faith; in fact, his orthodoxy is his pride and his glory;—*but yet he lives as if he did not believe a word of it.* Surely this man is practically insane. You cannot but regard such a case with horror. Oh! you say, if he had never known these things, he would not have incurred the guilt of this dreadful insanity; but, alas! he does know

them all. He has them all written down ;—all are
embraced in the standards of his faith, and he would
not be supposed to doubt one word of these standards
for the value of his best reputation. Then is he not
insane? Alas, the world is a complete bedlam! See
their manuals of doctrines ; read carefully their standards, and see what they believe ; then see how they live
—as if there were no heaven and no hell ; no atone-
ment, no Saviour ;—nothing but this world and its good
things! And are they not madmen? Does the Bible
slander them at all when it declares, " *Madness* is in
their heart while they live, and after that they go to
the dead "?

5. How must the people of other worlds look upon
the men of this! Particularly, I ask, how must they
regard those who live in those portions of our world
where light blazes and every eye must see it? How
are they astonished in heaven to see such exhibi-
tions of depravity on earth! How must they look
on with unutterable amazement as they mark the clear
and blazing light which God pours upon the realities
of the eternal world, and then observe how little this
light is regarded even by those who see it most and
best!

6. How many are struggling to secure any thing
and every thing else but the salvation of the soul! And
yet they know that every thing else gained is worse
than loss if the soul is lost. What egregious folly!
And, what is more, think of the appalling guilt! and
of the coming account to be rendered for both the guilt
and the folly! God will call you all to account—*you*

for the property you sought to the neglect of your soul, and chose at the cost of ruining your soul;—and *you* for the education which you valued more than the salvation of your soul. What, young man, do you propose to do with that education which you have put before your soul and sought to the neglect and ruin of your eternal being? You may enter the eternal world an educated young man—with all your powers developed and matured, so that you can take your position in that world of woe in an advanced class: as some young men come here prepared to enter in advance—as far perhaps as the junior year, so you, by virtue of your education, may enter among the more advanced minds in hell, ripe for drinking deeper draughts of remorse, your intellect enlarged for broader views of your relations, and sharpened for keener impressions of your fearful guilt! Oh what must it be to take your starting-point in that world of agonising thought, in advance of your age and your time, ready to start off with more rapid strides in the dread career of progression in the knowledge—in the sinning—and in the consequent woes of the damned! Take such a mind as Byron's. How much more is he capable of suffering in one hour on his death-bed than a mind of only ordinary capacity! Sit down by his death-bed; mark his rolling eye—his look of agony—the reach and grasp of his capacious soul! See how keenly he feels every sensation of remorse—how large his scope of view as he thinks of his relations to the God he should have loved but did not, and to the world he should have blessed by his talents but only cursed by his de-

pravity! You may have often said, if I were only as
great and as talented as Byron; if I only had his power
as a poet—his genius—his talent—how glorious! I
could ask nothing more.

You would then be as great as Byron! But what
then? Suppose you were; what would you gain?
What would it profit you to gain all he ever gained of
mental power, or earthly fame, and to lose your soul?
Oh think of this; to be a Byron and to lose your soul!
Would this be gain? Could you afford to devote your
being to such an object, and having gained it, die and
go to hell?

Or suppose you aspire to be a statesman. You
climb the slow assent of office; you rise in the confidence of your party, till step by step you ascend the
tall acclivity, and see the summit of ambition only a
little way before you : then down you go to hell! How
much have you gained, even if you have reached the
glittering summit, and then lose your soul?

7. In the eternal world there will be an entire reversal of position; the highest here are lowest there,
and the lowest here are the most favoured or certainly
the least accursed there. The kings of the earth, highest on their thrones, will have the largest account to
settle there, the heaviest responsibilities to bear, and of
course the most fearful doom. Here he sits in grand
and lofty state; the subject must kneel before him to
present even a petition; but death reverses the scene.
Let this king on his throne but die in his sins: he
tumbles from his rotten throne to the depths of hell!
Where does he go? What is his position among the

ranks of the lost? Down, deep in the lowest depths
of perdition. Here his princely steeds and outriding
footmen give him the *éclat* of nobility; but if he
abused his dignity to the feeding of earthly pride and
to the crushing of the poor, he sinks deep below those
once so far beneath him. Now they mark his fall like
Lucifer, son of morning. Now perhaps they hiss
at him, and curse him, saying, How art thou fallen
from the throne of thy glory! And thou art here,
down deep in the infamy of hell! Thou wretch! How
they hiss at all his plagues! The very fires of hell roar
and hiss at him as he sinks beneath their wild engulf-
ing billows. So the great ones of any country who sell
their souls for ambition and earthly power: what have
they gained? An office—it may be, a crown; but
they have lost a soul! Alas! where are they now?
The most miserably guilty and wretched among all the
wretched ones of hell! Hear what they say as they
go down wailing along the sides of the pit! " So much
for the folly of selling my soul for a bubble of vanity!
For an hour I sought and chose to be exalted; how
fearfully do I sink now, and sink for ever! Oh the contrast of earth and hell!" Hark! what do they say?
The man clothed in purple and fine linen lifts up his
eyes in hell, being in torments; he sees Abraham afar
off, and Lazarus, that old ulcerated beggar, is now in
his bosom; and what does he say? He cries aloud,
" Father Abraham, I pray thee send Lazarus to me;
let him dip only the tip of his finger in water and put
it on my tongue; I can do without my golden cup;
that's gone for ever now; but let Lazarus come with

his finger dipped in water and cool my tongue; for I am tormented in this flame ".

But what is the answer to this agonising prayer? Son, thou hast had thy good things, all of them, to the last dregs; and Lazarus all his evil things; now he is comforted and thou art tormented.

Let this illustrate what I mean in speaking of the wide but righteous *contrast* between the state of souls in time and in eternity; the strange reversal of condition, by which the lowest here become highest there, and the highest here become the lowest there.

8. Men really intend to secure both this world and salvation. They never suppose it wise to lose their own soul. Nor do they think to gain anything by running the risk of losing it. Indeed, they do not mean to run any great risks—only a little, the least they can conveniently make it, and yet gain a large measure of earthly good. But in attempting to get the world, they lose their souls. God told them they would, but they did not believe him. Rushing on the fearful venture and assuming to be wiser than God, they grasped the world to get it first, thinking to get heaven afterwards; thus they tempted the Spirit; provoked God to forsake them; lost their day of salvation and lost all the world besides. How infinitely just and right is their reward! Why did they not believe God? Every one of them knew that being saved through Christ, he would be infinitely rich, and being lost, he would make himself infinitely poor; and yet he rushed upon the fatal venture, and went down, despite of grace, to an eternal hell!

9.  What is really worth living for but to save souls? You may think it is worth living for to be a judge or a senator—but *is* it?   Is it, if the price must be the loss of your soul?   How many of our American Presidents have died as you would wish to die?   If you should live to gain the object of your ambition, what would be your chance of saving your soul?   The world being what it is, and the temptations incident to office and worldly honours being as they are, how great would be your prospects of saving your souls?   Would it be wise of you to run the hazard?

What else would you live for than to save souls? Would you not rather save souls than be President of this Union?   " He that winneth souls is wise."   " They that turn many to righteousness shall shine as the stars for ever."   Will this be the case with the ungodly Presidents who die in their sins?

What do you propose to do, young man, or young woman, with your education?   Have you any higher or nobler object to live for than to save souls?   Have you any more worthy object upon which to expend the resources of a cultivated mind and the accumulated powers gained by education?   Think—what should I live for but the gems of heaven—for what but the honour of Jesus, my Master?

They who do not practically make the salvation of souls—their own and others,—their chief concern, deserve not the name of rational; they are not sane. Look at their course of practical life as compared with their knowledge of facts.   Are they sane, or are they deranged?

It is time for the church to consecrate her mind and her whole heart to this subject. It is indeed time that she should lay these great truths in all their burning power close to her heart. Alas, how is her soul palsied with the spirit of the world! Nothing can save her and restore her to spiritual life until she brings her mind and heart into burning contact with these living, energising truths of eternity. The church of our times needs the apostolic spirit. She needs so deep a baptism with those fires of the Holy Ghost that she can go out and set the world on fire by her zeal for the souls of men. Till then the generation of our race must go on, thronging the broad way to hell because no man cares for their souls.

# 4

## GOD'S ANGER

" God is angry with the wicked every day."—*Psalms* vii. 11

In speaking from this text I design to show briefly :

    I. WHO ARE "WICKED" IN THE SCRIPTURE SENSE OF THIS TERM ;

    II. THAT GOD IS ANGRY WITH THEM ;

    III. THE NATURE OF THIS ANGER ;

    IV. THE REASONS FOR IT ;

    V. ITS DEGREE ;

    VI. ITS DURATION ;

    VII. THE TERRIBLE CONDITION OF SINNERS UNDER IT.

*1. The Bible divides all the human race into two classes only,—the righteous and the wicked.* Those are righteous who have true faith in Christ, whose spirit is consecrated to God, who live a heavenly life on earth, and who have been renewed by the Holy Ghost. Their original selfishness is subdued and slain and they live a new life through the ever-present grace of Christ Jesus.

Right over against them in character are the wicked, who have not been renewed in heart ; who live in self-ishness, under the dominion of appetite in some of its forms,—and it matters not in which, out of all possible

forms, it may be, but self is the great and only ultimate end of their life. These are, in the scriptural
sense, the wicked.

*II. God is angry with the wicked.* Our text explicitly affirms this. The same truth is affirmed and
implied in numerous other passages. Let the sinner
remember that this is the testimony of God himself.
Who should better know the feelings of God towards
sinners than God himself does? Who on this point
can gainsay what God affirms?

But this truth is also taught by reason. Every man
in the exercise of his reason knows it ought to be true.
If God were not opposed to the wicked, he would be
wicked himself for not opposing them. What would
you think of a judge who did not hate and oppose law-
breakers? Would you think him an honest man if he
did not take sides against transgressors? Everybody
knows that this is the dictate of reason and of common
sense. Sinners know this, and always assume it in
their practical judgments. They know that God is
angry with them, and ought to be—though they may
not realise it. Sinners know many things which they
do not realise. For instance, you who are in sin know
that you must die; but you have more reason to be
assured that God is angry with you than you have to
be sure that you must die; for it is not necessarily so
certain that you will die as it is that God is angry with
you for your sin. God may possibly translate you
from this world to another without your death, as he
has some others; but there never was, and never can
be, any exception to the universal law of his anger

against all the wicked. You know this, therefore, with an absolute certainty, which precludes all possibility of rational doubt.

Sinners do know this, as I have said, and always assume it in their practical judgments. Else why are they afraid to die? why afraid to meet God face to face in the world of retribution? Would they have this fear if they did not know that God is angry with them for their sin? It would be gratuitous, therefore, to *prove* this truth to the sinner. He already knows it—knows it not only as a thing that *is*, but as what *ought* to be.

*III. The nature of this anger demands our attention.* On this point it is important to notice negatively : —

1. It is not a malicious anger. God is never malicious ; never has a disposition to do any wrong in any way to any being. He is infinitely far from such feelings, and from any such developments of anger.

2. His anger is not passion in the sense in which men are wont to exhibit passion in anger. You may often have seen men whose sensibility is lashed into fury under an excitement of anger ; their very souls seem to be boiling with fermentation, so intense is their excitement. Reason for the time is displaced, and passion reigns. Now God is never angry in such a way. His anger against the wicked involves no such excitement of passion.

3. God's anger cannot be in any sense a selfish anger ; for God is not selfish in the least degree, but infinitely the reverse of it. Of course his anger against the wicked must be entirely devoid of selfishness.

But positively his anger against the wicked implies,

1. An entire disapprobation of their conduct and character. He disapproves most intensely and utterly everything in either their heart or their life. He loathes the wicked with infinite loathing.

2. He feels the strongest opposition of will to their character. It is so utterly opposed to his own character and to his own views of right that his will arrays itself in the strongest form of opposition against it.

3. God's anger involves also strong opposition of feeling against sinners. Undoubtedly God must have feelings of anger against the wicked. We cannot suppose it possible that God should behold sin without feelings of anger.

In our attempts to conceive of the mental faculties of the divine mind, we are under a sort of necessity of reasoning analogically from our own minds. Revelation has told us that we are "made in the image of God". Of course the mind of God is the antitype from which ours was cast. The great constituent elements of mind, we must suppose, are therefore alike in both the infinite and the finite. As we have intellect, sensibility, and will, so has God.

From our own minds, moreover, we infer not only what the faculties of the divine mind are, but also the laws under which they act. We know that in the presence of certain objects we naturally feel strong opposition. Those objects are so related to our sensibility that anger and indignation are the natural result. We could not act according to the fixed laws of our own minds if we did not utterly disapprove wrong-doing, and if our disapproval of it, moreover, did not awaken some real *sensibility* in the form of displeasure and indignation against the wrong-doer.

Some suppose that these results of the excited sensibility against wrong would not develop themselves if our hearts were right. This is a great mistake. The nearer right our hearts are, the more certainly shall we disapprove wrong, the more intensely shall we feel opposed to it, and the greater will be our displeasure against the wrong-doer. Hence we must not only suppose that God is angry in the sense of a will opposed to sin, but in the further sense of a sensibility enkindled against it. This must be the case if God is truly a moral agent.

4. God is not angry merely against the sin abstracted from the sinner, but against the sinner himself. Some persons have laboured hard to set up this ridiculous and absurd abstraction, and would fain make it appear that God is angry at the sin, yet not at the sinner. He hates the theft, but loves the thief. He abhors adultery, but is pleased with the adulterer. Now this is supreme nonsense. The sin has no moral character apart from the sinner. The act is nothing apart from the actor. The very thing that God hates and disapproves is not the mere event—the thing done in distinction from the doer ; but it is the *doer himself.* It grieves and displeases Him that a rational moral agent, under his government, should array himself against his own God and Father, against all that is right and just in the universe. This is the thing that

offends God. The sinner himself is the direct and the only object of his anger.

So the Bible shows. God is angry with the wicked, not with the abstract sin. If the wicked turn not, God will whet his sword,—he hath bent his bow and made it ready,—not to shoot the *sin*, however, but the *sinner* —the wicked man who has done the abominable thing. This is the only doctrine of either the Bible or of common sense on this subject.

5. The anger of God against the wicked implies all that properly belongs to anger when it exists *with good reason*. We know by our own experience that when we are angry with good reason, we have strong opposition of will, and also strong feelings of displeasure and disapprobation, against wrong-doers. Hence we may infer that under the same circumstances the same is true of God.

*IV*. The REASONS *of God's anger against the wicked next demand our attention*. His anger is never excited without good reasons. Causeless anger is always sinful. "Whoever is angry with his brother without a cause is in danger of the judgment." God never himself violates his own laws—founded as they are in infinite right and justice. Hence God's anger always has good reasons.

Good reasons exist for his anger, and he is angry for those reasons. It is not uncommon for persons to be angry, under circumstances, too, which are good reasons for anger, but still they are not angry for those good reasons, but for other reasons which are not good. For example, every sinner has good reasons for being

angry with every other sinner for his wickedness against
God. But sinners are not angry against other sinners
for those reasons. Although these reasons actually
exist, yet when angry at sinners, it is not for these
good reasons, but for some selfish reasons, which are
not good. This is a common case. You see persons
angry, and if you reprove them for their anger as sinful, they seek to justify themselves by affirming that
they are angry with the man for his sins—for his
wrong-doing against God. Now this is indeed a good
and sufficient reason for anger, and the justification
would be a good one if the anger were really excited by
this cause. But often, although this reason exists, and
is pleaded by the man as his excuse for anger, yet it is
no excuse, for, in fact, he is not angry for this cause,
but has some selfish reason for his anger. Not so with
God. God is angry with the wicked, not irrespective
of his sins, but for his sins.

1. Wicked men are entirely unreasonable. Their
conduct is at war with all reason and with all right.
God has given them intelligence and conscience; but
they act in opposition to both. God has given them
a pure and good law, yet this they recklessly violate.
Hence their conduct is in every point of view utterly
unreasonable.

Now we all know that, by a fixed law of our being,
nothing can be a greater temptation to anger than to
see persons act unreasonably. This is one of the
greatest trials that can occur, and one of the strongest
incentives to anger. So when God looks at the unreasonable conduct of sinners, he feels the strongest indig-

nation and displeasure. If they were not rational beings endowed with reason, no anger would be awak-
ened and called forth. But since God knows them to
be endowed with reason, and to be capable of true and
noble-hearted obedience, he cannot fail of being displeased with their transgression.

2. The course of the wicked is utterly ruinous. No
thanks to the sinner if his influence does not ruin the
whole world. By the very laws of mind, the sin of any
one man tends to influence other men to sin, and they
spread far and wide the dreadful contagion of his example. It may truly be said that the sinner does the
worst thing possible to him to ruin the universe. He
sets the example of rebellion against the supreme government of all worlds. And what influence can be
more potent than that of example? What worse thing,
therefore, can the sinner do to destroy all good than
he is doing by his sin? No thanks to him if every
man who sees his sin does not imitate it to his own
ruin, and throw the power of his own example broad-
cast over all his associates. No thanks to any sinner
if his own influence for ruin does not run like fire on
the prairies, over all the world, and then over every
other world of moral beings in the universe of God.

Think of the father of a family, living in his sins and
exerting his great influence over his household to make
them all as wicked as himself. Who can estimate the
power of his influence over his wife and his children?
Does he pray with them and seek to lead them to God?
No; his example is prayerless. It proclaims every day
to his family, "You have no occasion at all to pray.

You see I can live without prayer." Does he read the
Bible to them or with them? No; his constant example before them sets the Bible at naught, and continually suggests that they will be as well off without read-
ing the Bible as with. His whole influence, therefore,
is ruinous to the souls of his family. No thanks to
him, if they do not all go down to hell along with himself. If they do not scream around him with yells of
mingled imprecation and despair, cursing him as the
guilty author of their ruin, he will have other agencies
to thank besides his own. Surely he has done what
he well could do to secure results so dreadful as these.
Has not God good reason to be angry with him? Why
not? Would not you feel that you have good reasons
to be angry with a man who should come into your
family to destroy its peace—to seduce your wife and
daughters, and to entice your sons into some pathway
of crime and ruin? Certainly you would. Now do
not all families belong to God in a far higher sense
than any man's family belongs to him? Why, then,
has not God as good reasons for anger against a wicked
father as you could have against a villain who should
plot and seek to effect the mischief and ruin of your
family? Is it wonderful to you that God should be
angry with every wicked father? just consider what
that father is doing by his bare example—even supposing that his words are well-guarded and not particularly liable to objection. Who does not know that
example is the very highest and strongest moral power?
It does not need the help of teaching to make its
power felt for terrible mischief. The prayerless hus-

band and father! The devil could not do worse—nay,
more, not so bad ; for the devil never had mercy offered
him, never stood related as this wicked father does, to
offered pardon and to the glorious gospel. If, then,
God would have good reason to be angry at the devil,
much more has he for anger against this wicked father.

The same substantially is true of other classes of
sinners. It is essential to their very course as sinners,
that they are in rebellion against God, and are doing
the very worst thing in the universe by drawing other
moral beings into sin.

3. Again, God is so good and sinners are so wicked,
he cannot help being angry at them. If he were not
angry at the wicked, he would be as much worse than
they as he is wiser than they. Since, in his wisdom
and knowledge, he knows more fully than they do the
great evil of sin, by so much the more is he under
obligation to be displeased with sin and angry at the
sinner. We sometimes hear men say, " God is too
good to be angry at sinners ". What do men mean by
this language? Do they mean that God is too good
to be opposed to all evil? too good to be displeased
with all evil-doers ? This were indeed a strange goodness! God too good to hate sin—too good to oppose
sinners ! What sort of goodness can this be ?

I have sometimes heard men say that if God should
be angry with sinners, he would be as bad as the devil
himself. Now this is not only horrible language on the
score of its blasphemy, but it is monstrous absurdity
on the score of its logic. The amount of its logic is
that God would be himself wicked if he should be dis-

pleased at wickedness. So wrong it must be to hate
the wrong-doer! Pray, who is it that holds such doctrine? Is it not possible that they feel some interest
in sustaining wrong-doers even against God himself?

Really there is no force, no plausibility even, in this
language about the wrong of God's being angry at sinners, except what arises from misconceiving and mis-
representing the true idea of the divine anger in this
case. If God's anger were in itself sinful—as is the
case often with man's anger—then, of course, nothing
more can be said in its vindication. But since his anger is never sinful, never selfish, never malicious, never
unholy or wrong in any degree whatever, nothing can
be more false, nothing more sophistical, nothing more
ungenerous and vile and Satanic, than to imply that it
is. But this is just what men do when they say that
for God to be angry at sinners is to be himself wicked.

The true view of this case is not by any means ab-
struse or difficult of apprehension. Who does not
know that good men are, by virtue of their goodness,
opposed to wicked men? Surely all wicked men know
this well enough. Else why the fear they have of good
and law-abiding men? Why do all horse-thieves and
counterfeiters keep dark from good men,—dread their
presence,—commonly feel a strong dislike to them,
and always dread their influence as hostile to their own
wicked schemes?

So wicked men feel towards God. They know that
his goodness places him in hostile array against themselves. This fact seems to be implied in the Psalmist's
expostulation, "Why boastest thou thyself in mischief,

O mighty man? The goodness of God endureth continually." God is always good ; how can you be proud
of your wickedness? God is too good and too constantly good to afford you any scope for sin, any
ground of hope for peace with him in your iniquity.

*V. The degree of God's anger against sin should
be next considered.* It is plain that the degree of God's
anger against the wicked ought to be equal to the degree of their wickedness, and must be if God is what
he should be. The times of heathen ignorance and
darkness " God winked at"; the degree of their guilt
being less, by as much as their light is less, than that
of such cities as Chorazin and Bethsaida. God does
not hold them innocent *absolutely ;* but relatively they
might almost be called innocent, compared with the
great guilt of sinners in gospel lands. Against those
who sin amidst the clearest light, his anger must burn
most intensely ; for example, against sinners in this place
and congregation. You may be outwardly a decent
and moral man, respected and beloved by your friends ;
but if you are a selfish, impenitent sinner, the pure and
holy God loathes and abhors you. He sees more real
guilt in you than in ten thousand of those dark-minded
heathen who are bowing down to idol gods, and whose
crimes you read of with loathing and disgust. Think
of it. God may be more angry against you for your
great wickedness than against a nation of idolators
whose ignorance he winks at, while he measures your
light and consequent guilt in the balances of his own
eternal justice. Oh! are you living here amid the
blazing sunlight of truth ; knowing your duty every

day and every day refusing to do it; do you not know
that in the eye of God you are one of the wickedest
beings out of hell, or in hell, either, and that God's
hatred against your sin is equal to your great guilt?
But you say perhaps, Am I not moral and honest?
Suppose you are moral. *For whose sake* are you moral,
and for what reason? Is it not for your reputation's
sake only? The devil might be as moral for such a
purpose as you are. Mark, it is not for God's sake,—
not for Christ's sake,—that you are a moral man, but
because you love yourself. You might be just as
moral if there were no God, or if you were an atheist.
Of course if so, you are saying in your heart, Let there
be no fear of God before my eyes, no love of God in
my heart. Let me live, and have my own way, as if
there were no God. And all this you do, not under
the darkness of heathenism, but amid the broadest
sunlight of heaven's truth blazing all around you. Do
you still ask, What have I done? You have arrayed
yourself against God, rejected the gospel of his Son,
and done despite to the Spirit of his grace. What
heathen has ever done this, or anything that could
compare with this in guilt? The vilest heathen people
that ever wallowed in the filth of their own abominations are pure compared with you. Do you start back
and rebel against this view of your case? Then let us
ask again, By what rule are we to estimate guilt? You
pass along the street and you see the lower animals
doing what you would be horrified to see human beings
do, but you never think of them as *guilty*. You see
those dogs try to tear each other to pieces; you will

perhaps try to part them; but you will not think of feeling moral indignation or moral displeasure against them; and why? Because you instinctively judge of their guilt by their light, and by their capacity for governing themselves by light and reason. On nearly the same principle you might see the heathen reeking in their abominations, quarrelling, and practising the most loathsome forms of vice and selfishness; but their guilt is only a glimmering taper compared with yours, and therefore you cannot but estimate their guilt as by so much less than your own as their light is less! Your reason demands that you should estimate guilt on this principle, and you know that you cannot rightly estimate it on any other. For the very same reason you must conclude that God estimates guilt on the same principles, and that his anger against sin is in proportion to the sinner's guilt, estimated in view of the light he enjoys and sins against. The degree of God's anger against the wicked is not measured by their outward conduct, but by their real guilt as seen by him whose eye is on the heart.

*VI.* As to the *duration of God's anger against the wicked*, it manifestly must continue as long as the wickedness itself continues. As long as wicked men continue wicked, so long must God be angry at them every day. If they turn not, there can be no abatement, no cessation, of his anger. This is so plain that everybody must know it.

*VII. The terrible condition of the sinner against whom God is angry.*

This dreadful truth that God is angry with the

wicked every day, sinners know, but do not realize.
Yet it were well for you who are sinners to apprehend
and estimate this just as it is.

Look then at the attributes of God. Who and what
is God? Is he not a Being whose wrath against you
is to be dreaded? You often feel that it is a terrible
thing to incur the displeasure of some men. Children
are often exceedingly afraid of the anger of their parents. Any child has reason to feel that it is a terrible
state of things, when he has done wrong and knows
it must come to the knowledge of his father and his
mother, and must arouse their keenest displeasure
against himself—this is terrible, and no wonder a child
should dread it. How much more has the sinner reason to fear and tremble when by his sin he has made
the Almighty God his enemy! Think of his state!
Think of the case of the sinner's exposing himself to
the indignation of the great and dreadful God! Look
at God's natural attributes. Who can measure the
extent of his power? Who or what can resist his
will? He taketh up the isles as a very little thing,
and the nations before him are only as the small dust
of the balance. When his wrath is kindled, who can
stand before it, or stay its dreadful fury?

Think also of his omniscience. He knows all you
have done. Every act has passed underneath his eye ;
and not every external act, merely, but, what is far
more dreadful to you, every motive lying back of every
act—all the most hidden workings of your heart. Oh,
if you were only dealing with some one whom you
could deceive, how would you set yourself at work to

plan some deep scheme of deception! But all in vain
here, for God knows it all. If it were a case between
yourself and some human tribunal, you might cover up
many things; you might perjure yourself; or might
smuggle away the dreaded witnesses; but before God,
no such measures can avail you for one moment. The
whole truth will come out, dread its disclosure as much
as you may. The darkness and the light are both
alike to him, and nothing can be hidden from his eye.

Again, not only does God know everything you
have done, and not only is he abundantly able to punish you, but he is as much disposed as he is able, or
omniscient. You will find he has no disposition to
overlook your guilt. He is so good that he never can
let sin unrepented of pass unnoticed and unpunished.
It would be an infinite wrong to the universe if he
should! If he were to do it, he would at once cease
to be a good and holy God!

O sinner! do you ever think of God's perfect holiness the infinite purity of his heart? Do you ever
think how intensely strong must be his opposition to
your sin? to those sins of yours, which are so bad even
in your own view that you cannot bear to have many
of your fellow-men know them? How do you suppose your guilty soul appears in the eye of the pure
and holy God?

You often hear of God's mercy. You hope for some
good to yourself, perhaps, from this attribute of his
nature. Ah! if you had not spurned it, and trampled
it under your feet; if you had not slighted and abused
its manifestations to you, it might befriend you in your

day of need. But ah, how can you meet insulted
mercy! What can you say for yourself in defence for
having sinned against the richest mercy the world ever
saw? Can you hope that God's injured mercy will
befriend you? Nay, verily; God has not one attribute
which is not armed against you. Such is his nature,
and such his character, that you have nothing to hope,
but everything to fear. His dreadful anger against you
must be expressed. He may withhold its expression
for a season, to give the utmost scope for efforts to
reclaim and save you. But when these efforts shall
have failed, then will not justice take her course?
Will not insulted Majesty utter her awful voice? Will
not the infinite God arise in his awful purity, and proclaim, "I hate all wickedness, my anger burns against
the sinner to the lowest hell"? Will not Jehovah take
measures to make his true position towards sinners
known?

### CONCLUSION

1. God is much more opposed to sinners than Satan
is. Doubtless this must be so, for Satan has no special reason for being opposed to sinners. They are
doing his work very much as he would have them.
We have no evidence that Satan is displeased with their
course. But God is displeased with them, and for the
best of reasons.

Men sometimes say, If God is angry with the wicked,
he is worse than Satan. They seem to think that
Satan is a liberal, generous-hearted being. They are
rather disposed to commend him as, on the whole,
very charitable and noble-hearted. They may think

that Satan is bad enough, but they cannot be reconciled to it that God should be so hard on sinners.

Now the facts are that God is too good to be otherwise than angry with sinners. The devil is so bad himself that he finds no difficulty in being well enough pleased with their vileness : it does not offend him. Hence, from his very nature, God must hate the sinner infinitely more than Satan does.

2. If God were not angry with sinners, he would not be worthy of confidence. What would you think of a civil governor who should manifest no indignation against transgressors of the law ? You would say, of course, that he had not the good of the community at heart, and you could have no confidence in him.

3. God's anger with sinners is not inconsistent with his happiness. Why should it be, if it is not inconsistent with his holiness ? If there were anything wrong about it, then it would indeed destroy all his happiness ; but if it be intrinsically right, then it not only cannot destroy his happiness, but he could not be happy without anger against the wicked. His happiness must be conditioned upon his acting and feeling in accordance with the reality of things. Hence, if God did not hate sin and did not manifest his hatred in all proper ways, he could not respect himself ; he could not retire within the great deep of his own nature, and enjoy eternal bliss in the consciousness of infinite rectitude.

4. God's opposition to sinners is his glory. It is all-glorious to God to manifest his anger towards wicked men and devils. Is not this the fact with all good rulers ? Do they not seize every opportunity to

manifest their opposition to the wicked, and is not this
their real glory? Do we not account it their glory to
be zealous and efficient in detecting crime? Most certainly. They can have no other real glory. But suppose a ruler should sympathise with murderers, thieves,
robbers. We should execrate his very name!

5. Saints love God for his opposition to sinners,
not excepting even his opposition to their *own sins*.
They could not have confidence in him if he did not
oppose their own sins, and it is not in their hearts to
ask him to favour even their own iniquities. No;
where they come near him and see how he is opposed to their own sins, and to them on account of
them, they honour him and adore him the more.
They do not want any being in the universe to connive
at their own sins, or to take any other stand toward
themselves as sinners, than that of opposition.

6. This text is to be understood as it reads. Its
language is to be taken in its obvious sense. Some
have supposed that God is not really angry with sinners, but uses this language in accommodation to our
understandings.

This is an unwarrantable latitude of interpretation.
Suppose we should apply the same principle to what
is said of God's love. When we read, "God so loved
the world as to give his only begotten Son," suppose
we say, this cannot mean real love, such as we feel for
each other—no, nothing like this; the language is only
used by way of accommodation, and really has no particular sense whatever. This sort of interpretation
would destroy the Bible, or any other book ever writ-

ten.  The only sound view of this matter is that God
speaks as sensible men do—to be understood by the
reader and hearer, and of course uses language in its
most obvious sense.  If he says he is angry against
the wicked, we must suppose that he really is.

It is indeed true that we are to qualify the language,
as I have already shown, by what we absolutely know
of his real character, and therefore hence infer that this
language cannot imply malicious anger, or selfish anger,
or any forms of anger inconsistent with infinite benevolence.  But having made the necessary qualifications,
there are no more to be made, and the cardinal idea of
anger still remains—*a fixed eternal displeasure and op
position against all sinners because of their great guilt.*

7.  God's anger against the sinner does not exclude
love—real, compassionate love ; not, however, the love
of complacency, but the love of well-wishing and good-
willing ; not the love of him as a *sinner,* but the love
for him as a sentient being, who might be infinitely
happy in obedience to his God.  This is undoubtedly
the true view to be taken of God's attitude towards
sinners.  What parent does not know what this is?
You have felt the kindlings of indignation against the
wickedness of your child, but blended with this you
have also felt all the compassionate tenderness of a
parent's heart.

The sinner sometimes says, It cannot be that God is
angry with me, for he watches over me day by day ;
he feeds me from his table, and regales me with his
bounties.  Ah, sinner! you may be greatly mistaken
in this matter.  Don't deceive yourself!  God is slow

to anger indeed ; that is, he is slow to *give expression* to his anger, and himself assigns the reason, because he is long suffering towards sinners, " not willing that any should perish, but that all should come to repentance ". But take care that you do not misconceive his real feeling towards you. Beware, lest you misinterpret his great forbearance. He waits, I know; but the storm of vengeance is gathering. How soon he may come forth out of his place and unlock suddenly all the whirlwinds of his vengeance ! Ah, sinner ! this once done, they will sleep no more.

8. It is plain that sinners do not realise God's anger, though they know it. If they do both know and realise it, they manifest a degree of hardihood in iniquity which is dreadful. But the fact is, they keep the thought of God's anger from their minds. They are reckless about it, and treat it as they do death. Sinners know they must die, but they do not realise this fact. They do not love to sit down and commune with death—thinking how soon it may come, how certainly it will come; how the grave-worms will gnaw the flesh from their cheek-bones, and consume those eyes now bright and sparkling. These young ladies don't love to commune with such thoughts as these, and realise how soon these scenes will be realities.

So you don't love to think of God's anger against sin, of his reasons for his anger, and of his great provocations. You probably don't like to hear me preach about it, and yet I preach as mildly as I can. You can't bear to hear the subject brought forward and pressed upon your attention. Tell me, are you in the

habit of sitting down and considering this subject at-
tentively? If you were to do so, you could not con-
temn God and treat him as if you had no care for
him.

9. Are you aware, sinner, that you have made God
your enemy, and have you thought how terrible a
thing this is? Do you consider how impotent you are
to withstand God? If you were in any measure de-
pendent on any one of your fellow-men, you would not
like to make him your enemy. The student in this
college is careful not to make the faculty, or any one
of them, his enemy. The child has the same solici-
tude in regard to his parent. Now consider what you
are doing towards God—that God who holds your
breath in his hands, your very life, in his power. Let
him only withdraw his hand, and you sink to hell by
your own gravity. On a slippery steep you stand, and
the billows of damnation roll below! O sinner! are
you aware that when you lie down at night with your
weapons of rebellion against God in your very hands,
his blazing eye is on you? Are you well aware of
this?

You may recollect the case of a Mr. H., once a
student here. For a considerable time he had been
rebellious against the truth of God as presented here
to his mind, and this spirit of rebellion rose gradually
to a higher and yet higher pitch. It seemed to have
made about as much head as he could well bear, and
in this state he retired to bed, and extinguished his
light. All at once his room seemed full of dazzling
splendour; he gazed around; there stood before him a

glorious form—with eyes of unearthly and most searching power; gradually all else disappeared save one eye, which shone with indescribable brilliancy and seemed to search him through and through. The im-impression made on his mind was awful. Oh! said he, I could not have lived under it many minutes if I had not yielded and bowed in submission to the will of God.

Sinner, have you ever considered that God's searching eye is on *you*? Do you think of it whenever you lie down at night? If you should live so long and should lie down again on your bed, think of it then. Write it down on a little card, and hang it where it will most often catch your eye, " *Thou God seest me*". Do this; and then realise that God's eye is penetrating your very heart. Oh that searching, awful eye! You close your eyes to sleep—still God's eye is on you. It closes not for the darkness of night. Do you say, " I shall sleep as usual—I am not the sinner who will be kept awake through fear of God's wrath. Why should I be afraid of God? What have I to fear? I know indeed that God says 'Give me thy heart,' but I have no thought of doing it. I have disobeyed him many years and see no flaming wrath yet. I expect he will feed me still and fill my cup with every form of blessing "?

O sinner! for these very reasons have you the more cause to dread his burning wrath. You have abused his mercy well-nigh to the last moment of endurance. Oh, how soon will his wrath break forth against thee! and no arm in all the universe can stay its whelming floods of ruin. And if you don't believe it, its coming will be all the more sure, speedy, and awful!

# 5

## WHEN SIN IS FATAL

"Whosoever shall keep the whole law, and yet offend in one point is guilty of all."—*James* ii. 10

"He that is unjust in the least, is also unjust in much."—*Luke* xvi. 10.

IN speaking from these words, I inquire,

*I. What is it to persist in sin?*

1. To persist in sin is not to abandon it. If a person should only occasionally, under the force of temptation, fall into a sin, any form of sin, and should repent and abandon it for a time, and should only *occasionally* be overcome by a temptation to commit that form of sin, it would not be proper to say that he *persisted* in it; for, according to this supposition, he is not wilful, or obstinate, or habitual in the commission of this sin, but it is rather *accidental*, in the sense that the temptation *sometimes* overtakes and overcomes him, notwithstanding his habitual abandonment of it and resistance to it. But if the commission be *habitual*, a thing *allowed*, a thing indulged in habitually,—such a sin is persisted in.

2. A sin is persisted in, although it may not be outwardly repeated, if it be not duly confessed. An

**103**

individual may be guilty of a great sin, which he may
not repeat in the act ; nevertheless, while he neglects
or refuses to confess it, it is still on his conscience unrepented of, and, in that sense, is still persisted in.   If
the sin has been committed to the injury of some person or persons, and be not duly confessed to the par-
ties injured, it is still persisted in.

If any of you had slandered his neighbour to his
great injury, it would not do for you to merely abstain
from *repeating* that offence.   The sin is not abandoned
until it is confessed, and reparation made, so far as
confession can make it.   If not confessed, the injury is
allowed to work ; and therefore the sin is virtually
repeated, and therefore persisted in.

Again, 3.   A sin is persisted in when due reparation has not been made.   If you have wronged a person, and it is in your power to make him restitution
and satisfaction, then, so long as you persist in neglecting or refusing to do so, you do not forsake the
sin, but persist in it.   Suppose one who had stolen
your property, resolved never to repeat the act, and
never to commit the like again ; and yet he refuses
to make restitution and restore the stolen property as
far as is in his power ;—of course he still persists in
that sin, and the wrong is permitted to remain.

I once had a conversation with a young man to this
effect.   He had been in the habit of stealing.   He
was connected with a business in which it was possible
for him to steal money in small sums, which he had
repeatedly done.   He afterwards professed to become
a Christian, but he made no restitution.   He found in

the Bible this text, " Let him that stole steal no more".
He resolved not to steal any more, and there let the
matter rest.  Of course he had no evidence of acceptance with God, for he could not have been accepted.
However he flattered himself that he was a Christian
for a long time, until he heard a sermon on confession
and restitution, which woke him up.  He then came
to me for the conversation of which I have spoken.

He was told that, if it was in his power, he must
make restitution and give back the stolen money, or
he could not be forgiven.  But observe his perversion
of Scripture.  To be sure it is the duty of those who
have stolen property to steal no more ; but this is not
all.  He is bound to restore that which he has stolen,
as well as to steal no more.  This is a plain doctrine
of Scripture, as well as of reason and conscience.

*II.*  I now come to the main doctrine of our texts
—that *any one form of sin persisted in is fatal to the
soul.*

That is, it is impossible for a person to be saved
who continues to commit any form of known sin.

1.  It is fatal to the soul because any one form of
sin persisted in is a violation of the spirit of the whole
law.  The text in James settles that :  " Whosoever
shall keep the whole law, and yet offend in one point,
is guilty of all ".  The law requires supreme love to
God, and equal love to our fellow-men.

Now sin is selfishness ; and always assumes the pref-
erence of self-interest and self-gratification to obedience to God, or to our duty to our fellow-men.

Whosoever, therefore, habitually prefers himself to

God, or is selfish in regard to his fellow-men, cannot
be a Christian. If in any one thing he violates the
law of love, he breaks the spirit of the whole law, and
is living in sin.

2.   Persistence in any form of sin cannot consist with
supreme love to God or equal love to our fellow-men.
If we love God more than ourselves, we cannot dis-
oblige him for the sake of obliging ourselves. We cannot displease him, knowingly and habitually, for the
sake of pleasing ourselves.

For we supremely love whom we supremely desire
to please. If we supremely desire to please ourselves,
we love ourselves supremely. If we love God supremely, we desire supremely to please him ; and cannot,
consistently with the existence of this love in the soul,
consent to displease him.

Under the force of a powerful temptation that diverts and partially distracts the mind, one who loves
God may be induced to commit an *occasional* sin, and
*occasionally* to displease God.

But if he love God supremely, he will consent to
displease him only under the pressure of a present and
powerful temptation that diverts attention and partially distracts the mind. So that his sin cannot be
*habitual;* and no form of sin can habitually have dominion over him if he is truly a Christian.

3.   The text in James affirms the impossibility of
real obedience in one thing, and of persistent disobedience in another, at the same time. It seems to me a
great and common error to suppose that persons can
really obey God in the spirit of obedience in *some*

things, while at the same time there are certain other things in which they withhold obedience; in other words, that they can obey one commandment and disobey another at the same time—that they can perform one duty acceptably, and at the same time refuse to perform other duties.

Now the text in James is designed flatly to contradict this view of the subject. It asserts as plainly as possible, that disobedience in any one point is wholly inconsistent with true obedience, for the time being, in any other respect; that the neglect of one duty renders it impossible, for the time being, to perform any other duty with acceptance; in other words, no one can obey in one thing and disobey in another at the same time.

But 4.    Real obedience to God involves and implies supreme regard for his authority.

Now if any one has a supreme regard for God's authority in any one thing, he will yield to his authority in everything.

But if he can consent to act against the authority of God in any one thing for the time being, he cannot be accepted in anything; for it must be that, while in one thing he rejects the authority of God, he does not properly accept it in any other.    Hence, if obedience to God be real in *anything*, it extends for the time being, and *must* extend, to *everything known to be the will of God*.

Again, 5.    One sin persisted in is fatal to the soul, because it is a real rejection of God's *whole* authority. If a man violates knowingly any one of God's com-

mandments as such, he rejects the authority of God ;
and if in this he rejects the authority of God, he rejects
his *whole* authority, for the time being, on every subject.    So that if he *appears* to obey in other things
while in one thing he sets aside and contemns God's
authority, it is only the *appearance* of obedience, and
not *real* obedience.   He acts from a *wrong motive* in
the case in which he appears to obey.   He certainly
does not act out of supreme respect to God's authority ; and therefore he does not truly obey him.   But
surely one who rejects the whole authority of God cannot be saved.

I fear it is very common for persons to make a fatal
mistake here ; and really to suppose that they are accepted in their obedience in general, although in some
things or thing they habitually neglect or refuse to do
their duty.

They live, and *know* that they live, in the omission
of some duty habitually, or in the violation of their
own consciences on some point habitually ; and yet
they keep up so much of the form of religion, and do
so many things that they call duties, that they seem to
think that these will compensate for the sin in which
they persist.   Or rather, so many duties are performed,
and so much of religion is kept up, as will show, they
think, that upon the whole they are Christians ; will
afford them ground for hope, and give them reasons to
think that they are accepted while they are indulging,
and *know* that they are, in some known sin.

They say, To be sure, I know that I neglect that
duty ; I know that I violate my conscience in that

thing ; but I do so many other things that are my duty, that I have good reason to believe that I am a Christian.

Now this is a fatal delusion. Such persons are totally deceived in supposing that they really obey God in anything. " He that is unjust in the least, is really unjust also in much ; " and " whosoever will keep the whole law, and yet offend in one point, is guilty of all ".

Again, 6. Any form of sin persisted in is fatal to the soul, because it is inconsistent with true repentance. Sin, however great, will be forgiven if repented of. But what *is* repentance ? Repentance is not mere sorrow for sin, but it is the *heart* renunciation of sin ; it is the giving up of sin from the heart, and of all sin as sin ; it is the rejection of it because it is that abominable thing which God hates ; it is the turning of the heart from self-seeking to supreme love to God and equal love to our fellow-men ; it is *heart*-reformation ; it is *heart*-rejection of sin ; it is *heart*-turning to God. Now, while any one sin is persisted in and not given up, there can be no true repentance ; for, after all, this form of sin is preferred to the will of God—the indulgence of sense in this particular is preferred to pleasing God. There can, therefore, be no true repentance unless all known sin be for the time utterly abandoned.

7. Persistence in any form of sin is fatal to the soul, because it is utterly inconsistent with *saving faith*. That faith is saving which actually *does* save from sin ; and no other faith is saving or *can* be. That faith is *justifying* which is *sanctifying*. True faith works by love ; it purifies the heart ; it overcomes the world.

These are expressly affirmed to be the characteristics of saving faith. Let no one suppose that his faith is justifying, when, in fact, it does not save him from the commission of sin ; for he cannot be justified while he persists in the commission of any known sin. If his faith does not purify his heart, if it does not overcome the world and overcome his sins, it can never save him.

Again, 8. Persistence in any one form of sin is fatal to the soul, because it withstands the power of the gospel. The gospel does not save whom it does not sanctify. If sin in any form withstands the saving power of the gospel ; if sin does not yield under the influence of the gospel ; if it be persisted in, in spite of all the power of the gospel on the soul ; of course the gospel does not, *cannot*, save that soul. Such sin is fatal.

But again, 9. Persistence in any one form of sin is fatal to the soul, because the grace of the gospel cannot pardon what it cannot eradicate.

As I have already said, a sin cannot be pardoned while it is persisted in. Some persons seem to suppose that, although they persist in many forms of sin, yet the grace of God will pardon sins that it has not power to eradicate and subdue. But this is a great mistake. The Bible everywhere expressly teaches this —that if the gospel fails to eradicate sin, it can never save the soul from the consequences of that sin.

But again, 10. If the gospel should pardon sin which it did not eradicate, this would not save the soul.

Suppose God should not punish sin ; still, if the soul be left to the self-condemnation of sin, its salvation is naturally impossible.  It were of no use to the sinner to be pardoned, if left under this self-condemnation. This is plain.  Let no one, therefore, think that, if his sins are not subdued by the grace of the gospel, he can be saved.

But again, 11, and lastly.  Sin is a *unit* in its *spirit* and *root*.  It consists in preferring self to God.

Hence, if any form of preferring self to God be persisted in, no sin has been truly abandoned ; God is not supremely loved ; and the soul cannot, by any possibility, in such a case, be saved.

## CONCLUSION

1.  What a *delusion* the self-righteous are under.

Every man is aware that he has sinned at some time, and that he is a sinner.  But there are many who think that, upon the whole, they perform so many good deeds, that they are safe.  They are aware that they are habitually neglecting God and neglecting duty, that they neither love God supremely nor their neighbour as themselves ; yet they are constantly prone to give themselves credit for a great deal of goodness. Now let them understand that there is no particle of righteousness in them, nor of true goodness, while they live in neglect of any known duty to man—while they are constantly prone to give themselves credit for a great deal of goodness.  But they seem to think that they have a balance of good deeds.

2. How many persons indulge in little sins, as they call them; but they are too *honest*, they think, to indulge in great crimes. Now both these texts contradict this view. "He that is unjust in that which is least, is unjust also in much." If a man yields to a slight temptation to commit what he calls a small sin, it cannot be a regard for God that keeps him from committing great sins. He may abstain from committing great sins through fear of disgrace or of punishment, but not because he loves God. If he does not love God well enough to keep from yielding to slight temptations to commit small sins, surely he does not love him well enough to keep from yielding to great temptations to commit great sins.

Again, 3. We see the delusion of those who are guilty of habitual dishonesties, tricks of trade for example, and yet profess to be Christians.

How many are there who are continually allowing themselves to practise little dishonesties, little deceptions, and to tell little lies in trade ; and yet think themselves Christians ! Now this delusion is awful ; it is fatal. Let all such be on their guard, and understand it.

But again, 4. We see the delusion of those professors of religion who allow themselves habitually to neglect some known duty, and yet think themselves Christians. They shun some cross ; there is something that they know they ought to do which they do not, and this is habitual with them. Perhaps all their Christian lives they have shunned some cross, or neglected the performance of some duty, and yet they

think themselves Christians. Now let them know
assuredly that they are *self-deceived*.

5. Many, I am sorry to say, preach a gospel that
is a dishonour to Christ. They really maintain,—at
least they make this impression, though they may not
teach it in words and form,—that Christ really justifies
men while they are living in the habitual indulgence of
known sin.

Many preachers seem not to be aware of the impression which they really leave upon their people. Probably, if they were asked whether they hold and preach
that any sin is forgiven which is not repented of ;
whether men are really justified while they persist in
known sin, they would say, No. But, after all, in their
preaching, they leave a very different impression. For
example, how common it is to find ministers who are
in this position : You ask them how many members
they have in their church. Perhaps they will tell you,
Five hundred. How many, do you think, are living up
to the best light which they have ? How many of
them are living from day to day with a conscience void
of offence toward God and toward man, and are not
indulging in any known sin either of omission or commission ? who are living and aiming to discharge punc-
tually and fully every duty of heart to God and to all
their fellow-men ? Push the inquiry, and ask, How
many of your church can you honestly say, before
God, you think are endeavouring to live without sin ?
who do not indulge themselves in any form of transgression or omission ?

They will tell you, perhaps, that they do not know

a member of their church, or at least they know but
very few, of whom they can say this.  Now ask them
further, How many of your church do you suppose to
be in a state of justification?  and you will find that
they have the impression that the great mass of their
church are in a state of justification with God ; in a
state of acceptance with him ;  in a state in which they
are prepared to die ;  and if they should die just in this
state by any sudden stroke of Providence, and they
should be called upon to preach their funeral sermon,
they would assume that they had gone to heaven.

While they will tell you that they know of but very
few of their church of whom they can conscientiously
say, I do not believe he indulges himself in any known
sin ; yet, let one of that great majority, of whom he
cannot say this, suddenly die, and this pastor be called
to attend his funeral, would he not comfort the mourn-
ers by holding out the conviction that he was a Christian, and had gone to heaven?  Now this shows that
the pastor himself, whatever be his theoretical views of
being justified while indulging in any known sin, is yet,
after all, practically an antinomian ;  and practically
holds, believes, and teaches that Christ justifies people
while they are living in the neglect of known duty,
while they are knowingly shunning some cross, while
they persist in known sin.  Ministers, indeed, often
leave this impression upon their churches (and I fear
*Calvinistic* ministers quite generally), that if they are
converted, or ever *were*, they are justified, although
they may be living habitually and always in the indulgence of more or less known sin,—living in the habitual

neglect of known duty, indulging various forms of selfishness. And yet they are regarded as justified Christians: and get the impression, even from the preaching of their ministers, that all is well with them ; that they really believe the gospel and are saved by Christ.

Now this is really antinomianism. It is a faith without law ; it is a Saviour that saves *in* and not *from* sin. It is presenting Christ as really setting aside the moral law and introducing another rule of life; as forgiving sin while it is persisted in, instead of saving *from* sin.

6. Many profess to be Christians, and are indulging the hope of eternal life, who know that they never have forsaken all forms of sin ; that in some things they have always fallen short of complying with the demands of their own consciences. They have indulged in what they call *little* sins ; they have allowed themselves in practices, and in forms of self-indulgence, that they cannot justify ; they have never reformed all their bad habits, and have never lived up to what they have regarded as their whole duty. They have never really *intended* to do this; have never resolutely set themselves, in the strength of Christ, to give up every form of sin, both of omission and commission; but, on the contrary, they know that they have always indulged themselves in what they condemn. And yet they call themselves Christian ! But this is as contrary to the teaching of the Bible as possible. The Bible teaches, not only that men are condemned by God if they indulge themselves in what they condemn ; but, also,

that God condemns them if they indulge in that the lawfulness of which they so much as *doubt*. If they indulge in any one thing the lawfulness of which is in their own estimation doubtful, God condemns them. This is the express teaching of the Bible. But how different is this from the common ideas that many professors of religion have !

7. Especially is this true of those who habitually indulge in the neglect of known duties, and who habitually shun the cross of Christ. Many persons neglect family prayer, and yet admit that they ought to perform it. How many females will even stay away from the female prayer-meeting to avoid performing the duty of taking a part in those meetings ! How many indulge the hope that they are saved, while they know that they are neglecting, and always *have* neglected, some things, and even *many* things, that they admit to be their duty ! They continue to live on in those omissions ; but they think they are Christians because they do not engage in anything that is openly disgraceful, or, as they suppose, very bad.

Now there are many that entirely overlook the real nature of sin. The law of God is *positive*. It commands us to consecrate all our powers to his service and glory ; to love him with all our heart and our neighbour as ourself. Now to neglect to do this is sin ; it is positive transgression ; it is an omission which always involves a *refusal* to do what God requires us to do. In other words, sin is the *refusal* to do what God requires us to do. It is the neglect to fulfil our obligations. If one neglects to pay you what he owes you, do you not call that sin, especially if the neglect involves necessarily the refusal to pay when he has the means of payment?

Sin really consists in withholding from God and man that love and service which we owe them—a withholding from God and man their due.

Now, where any one withholds from God and man what is their due, is this honest? is this Christian? And while this withholding is persisted in, can an individual be in a *justified* state? No, indeed!

The Bible teaches that sin is forgiven when it is repented of, but never while it is persisted in. The Bible teaches that the grace of God can save us *from* sin—from the *commission* of sin, or can pardon when we repent and put away sin; but it never teaches that sin can be forgiven while it is persisted in.

Let me ask you who are here present, Do you think you are Christians? Do you think, if you should die in your present state, that you are prepared to go to heaven? that you are already justified in Christ?

Well now, let me further ask, Are you so much as seriously and solemnly *intending* to perform to Christ, from day to day, your whole duty, and to omit nothing that you regard as your duty either to God or man? Are you not habitually shunning some cross? *omitting* something because it is a trial to perform that duty? Are you not avoiding the performance of *disagreeable* duties, and things that are trying to flesh and blood? Are you not neglecting the souls of those around you? Are you not failing to love your neighbour as yourself? Are you not neglecting something that you yourself confess to be your duty? and is not this *habitual* with you?

And now, do you suppose that you are really to be saved while guilty of these neglects habitually and persistently? I beg of you, be not deceived.

8. The impression of many seems to be, that grace will *pardon* what it cannot *prevent;* in other words, that if the grace of the gospel fails to save people from the *commission* of sin in this life, it will nevertheless, pardon them and save them *in* sin, if it cannot save *from* sin.

Now, really, I understand the gospel as teaching that men are saved *from* sin *first*, and, as a consequence, from hell ; and not that they are saved from hell while they are not saved from sin. Christ sanctifies when he saves. And this is the very first element or idea of salvation, saving *from* sin. " Thou shalt call his name Jesus," said the angel, " for he shall save his people *from their sins*." " Having raised up his Son Jesus," said the apostle, "he hath sent him to bless you in turning every one of you from his iniquities."

Let no one expect to be saved from hell, unless the grace of the gospel saves him first from sin.

Again, 9. There are many who think that they truly *obey* God in *most* things, while they know that they habitually *disobey* Him in *some* things. They seem to suppose that they render acceptable obedience to *most* of the commandments of God, while they are aware that *some* of the commandments they habitually disregard. Now the texts upon which I am speaking, expressly deny this position, and plainly teach that if in any one thing obedience is refused, if any one commandment is disobeyed, no other commandment is acceptably obeyed, or can be for the time being.

Do let me ask you who are here present, Is not this impression in your minds that, upon the whole, you have evidence that you are Christians?

You perform so many duties and avoid so many outbreaking sins; you think that there is so great a balance in your favour,—that you obey so many more commands than you disobey,—that you call yourselves Christians, although you are aware that some of the commandments you never seriously *intended* to comply with, and that in some things you have always allowed yourself to fall short of known duty. Now, if this impression is in your minds, remember that it is not authorised at all by the texts upon which I am speaking, nor by any part of the Bible. You are really disobeying the spirit of the whole law. You do not truly embrace the gospel; your faith does not purify your heart and overcome the world; it does not work by love, and therefore it is a *spurious* faith, and you are yet in your sins. Will you consider this? Will you take home this truth to your inmost soul?

10. There are many who are deceiving themselves by indulging the belief that they are forgiven, while they have not made that confession and restitution which is demanded by the gospel. In other words, they have not truly repented; they have not given up their sin. They do not outwardly *repeat* it; neither do they in heart forsake it.

They have not made restitution ; and therefore they hold on to their sin, supposing all is right if they do not repeat it ; that Christ will forgive them while they make no satisfaction, even while satisfaction is in their power. This is a great delusion, and is greatly dishonouring to Christ. As if Christ would disgrace himself by forgiving you while you persist in doing your neighbour wrong !

This he cannot do ; this he will not, must not do. He loves your neighbour as really as he loves you. He is infinitely willing to forgive provided you repent and make the restitution in your power ; but until then, he cannot, will not.

I must remark again, 11. That from the teachings of these texts it is evident that no one truly *obeys* in any *one* thing, while he allows himself to *disobey* in any *other* thing. To obey God truly in anything, we must settle the question of universal obedience ; else all our pretended obedience is vain. If we do not yield the *whole* to God ; if we do not go the whole length of seriously giving up all, and renouncing in heart *every form* of sin, and make up our minds to obey him in *everything*, we do not truly obey him in anything.

Again, 12. From this subject we can see why there are so many professors of religion that get no peace, and have no evidence of their acceptance. They are full of doubts and fears. They have no religious enjoyment, but are groping on in darkness and doubt ; are perhaps praying for evidence and trying to get peace of mind, but fall utterly short of doing so.

Now, in such cases you will often find that some known sin is indulged; some known duty continually neglected; some known cross shunned; something avoided which they know to be their duty, because it is trying to them to fulfil their obligation. It is amazing to see to what an extent this is true.

Some time since, an aged gentleman visited me, who came from a distance as an inquirer. He had been a preacher, and indeed was then a minister of the gospel; but he had given up preaching because of the many doubts that he had of his acceptance with Christ. He was in great darkness and trouble of mind; had been seeking religion, as he said, a great part of his life; and had done everything, as he supposed, in his power, to obtain evidence of his acceptance.

When I came to converse with him, I found that there were sins on his conscience that had been there for many years; plain cases of known transgression, of known neglect of duty indulged all this while. Here he was, striving to get peace, striving to get evidence, and even abandoning preaching because he could not get evidence; while all the time these sins lay upon his conscience. Amazing! amazing!

Again, 13. I remark, That total abstinence from all known sin is the only practicable rule of life. To sin in one thing and obey in another at the same time is utterly impossible. We must give up, in heart and purpose, *all* sin, or we in reality give up *none*. It is utterly impossible for a man to be truly religious *at all*, unless in the purpose of his heart he is *wholly* so and *universally* so. He cannot be a Christian at home

and a sinner abroad; or a sinner at home and a Christian abroad.

He cannot be a Christian on the Sabbath, and a
selfish man in his business or during the week. A
man must be one or the other; he must yield *everything* to God, or in fact he yields *nothing* to God.

He cannot serve God and mammon. Many are trying to do so, but it is impossible. They cannot love
both God and the world; they cannot serve two mas-
ters; they cannot please God and the world. It is the
greatest, and yet the most common, I fear, of all mis-
takes, that men can be truly but knowingly only *partially* religious; that in some things they can truly
yield to God, while in other things they refuse to obey
him. How common is this mistake! If it is not,
what shall we make of the state of the churches?
How are we to understand the great mass of professors? How are we to understand the great body of
religious teachers, if they do not leave the impression,
after all, on the churches, that they can be accepted
of God while their habitual obedience is only very
partial; while, in fact, they pick and choose among
the commandments of God, professing to obey some,
while they allow themselves in known disobedience of
others. Now, if in this respect the church has not a
false standard; if the mass of religious instruction is
not making a false impression on the churches and on
the world in this respect, I am mistaken. I am sorry to
be obliged to entertain this opinion, and to express it;
but what else can I think? How else can the state of
the churches be accounted for? How else is it that

ministers hope that the great mass of their churches
are in a safe state? How else is it that the great mass
of professors of religion can have any hope of eternal
life in them, if this is not the principle practically
adopted by them, that they are justified while only
rendering habitually but a very partial obedience to
God ; that they are really forgiven and justified while
they only pick and choose among the commandments,
obeying those which it costs them little to obey, and
are not disagreeable and not unpopular ; while they do
not hesitate habitually to disobey where obedience
would subject them to any inconvenience, require self-
denial, or expose them to any persecution ?

Again, 14. From what has been said, it will be seen
that *partial reformation* is no evidence of *real conversion*. Many are deceiving themselves on this point.
Now we should never allow ourselves to believe that a
person is converted if we perceive that his reformation
extends to certain things only, while in certain other
things he is not reformed ; especially when, in the case
of those things in which he is not reformed, he admits
that he ought to perform those duties, or to relinquish
those practices. If we find him still persisting in what
he himself admits to be wrong, we are bound to assume
and take it for granted that his conversion is not real.

Again, 15. Inquirers can see what they must do.

They must abandon *all* sin ; they must give up *all*
for Christ : they must turn with their whole heart and
soul to him ; and must make up their minds to yield
a full and hearty obedience as long as they live. They
must settle this in their minds ; and must cast them-

selves upon Christ for forgiveness for all the past, and grace to help in every time of need for the future. Only let it be settled in your mind fully that you will submit yourself to the whole will of God; and then you may expect, and are bound to expect, him to forgive all the past, however great your sins may have been.

You can see, Inquirer, why you have not already obtained peace. You have prayed for pardon; you have prayed for peace; you have endeavoured to get peace, while, in fact, you have not given up all; you have kept something back. It is a perfectly common thing to find that the inquirer has not given up all. And if you do not find peace, it is because you have not given up all.

Some idol is still retained; some sin persisted in—perhaps some neglect—perhaps some confession is not made that ought to have been made, or some act of restitution. You have not renounced the world, and do not, in fact, renounce it, and renounce everything, and flee to Christ.